Teaching Christianity

AT KEY STAGE 2

The Christian journey

Lilian Weatherley and Trevor Reader

Illustrations by Claire Foley

The National Society
*Leading Education
with a Christian Purpose*
Church House Publishing

This book is dedicated to our children,
Sam, Kris, Alex, Kate, Susie
and Lucy Reader and Stephen Weatherley

The National Society/Church House Publishing
Church House
Great Smith Street
London SW1P 3NZ

ISBN 0 7151 4943 1

Published 2001 by National Society Enterprises Ltd

Cover design and icons by Leigh Hurlock

Typeset in Sabon 11 point

Printed by The Cromwell Press Ltd, Trowbridge, Wiltshire

Contents

Acknowledgements

We should like to thank all those people who have given us so much help and support during the course of producing this book:

Our families, Lesley and John for their unending patience and perseverance during the writing of this book. Without their support, reading and encouragement it would not have been possible;

Alison Seaman and Alan Brown for their patience in reading the manuscript, as well as their advice, creative ideas and suggestions;

Revd Hugh Williams and Revd Canon Doctor John Cullen for their theological insight and suggestions;

The Winchester Museum services, Mrs Joyce West for her loan of her family photograph of the funeral of her uncle, Thomas Carpenter (p. 71) and Mr John Crook for his photograph of Winchester Cathedral nave (p. 59).

The publisher gratefully acknowledges permission to reproduce copyright material in this book. Every effort has been made to trace and contact copyright holders. If there are any inadvertent omissions we apologize to those concerned and undertake to include suitable acknowledgements in all future editions.

All biblical quotations in this book are taken from the *New Revised Standard Version*.

The profession of faith from the Baptism service in *Common Worship: Services and Prayers for the Church of England* (Church House Publishing, 2000) and the Apostles Creed from the Funeral service in *Common Worship: Pastoral Services* (Church House Publishing, 2000), based (or excerpted) from *Praying Together* © ELLC, 1988 are reproduced by permission of the publishers.

Other extracts from *Common Worship: Initiation Services* (Church House Publishing, 1998), *Common Worship: Services and Prayers for the Church of England* (Church House Publishing, 2000) and *Common Worship: Pastoral Services* (Church House Publishing, 2000), are copyright © The Archbishops' Council and are reproduced by permission.

Introduction

In recent years the emphasis on raising standards in education has made increasing demands on primary teachers. The majority of primary teachers who are not specialist teachers in Religious Education (RE) have had to work hard to develop their own subject knowledge in order to offer a curriculum that is filled with rigour and challenge for the children.

It is clear from working with teachers and delivering in-service training that many teachers still lack the necessary background knowledge to enable them to teach RE successfully. For example, at a recent course exploring the Christmas story, the majority of primary teachers present thought that the Christmas story was to be found in each gospel and that there were three wise men in Matthew's account of the Epiphany story. Recent Ofsted and Section 23 inspection reports have also highlighted the lack of specialist knowledge at Key Stage 2, especially in areas where there are large proportions of talented and more able pupils.

This book aims to provide teachers with some essential background information. Although the overall structure is the same as that of its sister book *Teaching Christianity at Key Stage* 1 the emphasis is on giving the non-specialist teacher more background information and, where necessary, help with the theology surrounding the themes chosen. As with *Teaching Christianity at Key Stage* 1, we have attempted to include the range of Christian denominations. The primary focus, however, is on the beliefs and practices of the Church of England, enabling teachers to use these as a way of comparing and contrasting with other Christian denominations. This is a key element of the majority of Agreed Syllabus documents at Key Stage 2 and a key skill for more able pupils.

We have chosen the theme of **journeys** as our central focus because for Christians life is a journey of faith which begins at baptism. Each section follows the same format as the Key Stage 1 book. It begins by offering informative background material for the teacher and this is followed by the main teaching ideas, ways in which the Bible can help and a selection of activities which motivate and challenge the children at this level. Finally as with the Key Stage 1 book there is a thought-provoking question for the children entitled **Something to think about**.

A journey through the gospels provides the non-specialist teacher at Key Stage 2 with a simple theological background to the gospels.

A journey through the Church past and present takes a brief look at the history of the Christian Church and can be linked in to some of the history topics such as the Romans, the Tudors and the Victorians.

A journey through the Church year explores the Church's year and can be a useful source of information not only for RE but also for collective worship and topics on the local community.

The Christian journey through life examines some key aspects of the Christian journey of life. It begins with baptism and ends with funeral rites and Christian belief about life after death.

A journey to a church has a slightly different approach. It follows on from the section 'Visiting a church' in *Teaching Christianity at Key Stage* 1 but with the focus on the senses and their importance in spiritual development and Christian worship.

Ideas are suggested as to how teachers might explore a Christian church with children when it is empty and also during worship.

In May 2000 The Qualifications and Curriculum Authority (QCA) published its new guidance on RE. Although schools will be following the requirements of their Local Agreed Syllabus or

Diocesan Syllabus and Guidelines in the case of Aided Schools, the QCA material does however offer an additional support and an opportunity for RE to be viewed as the statutory subject which it has always been.

The following units of work on Christianity at Key Stage 2 are covered by the QCA material:

What do signs and symbols mean in religion?

What do we know about Jesus?

What is the Bible and why is it important for Christians?

What is faith and what difference does it make?

Celebrations: Christmas journeys

Why is Easter important to Christians?

What religions are represented in our neighbourhood?

Where did the Bible come from?

How do the beliefs of Christians influence their actions?

Worship and community (generic)

Why are sacred texts important? (generic)

What can we learn from Christian religious buildings?

How do people express their faith through the arts?

Teaching Christianity at Key Stage 2 will enable teachers to have detailed background information to cover each of these units. The use of Christian signs and symbols throughout the book and the final section explaining these will also be of great value in extending teachers' knowledge of the range of Christian signs and symbols.

A journey through the gospels

Background to the gospels

It will help to know . . .

What is a gospel?

The word 'gospel' is derived from the Old English words *god spel* which meant 'good news', and going back even further in time, it came from the Old Greek word *evangelion*. Roman emperors used the word *evangelion* frequently but in their day they used it in a plural sense. Thus the Emperor's birthday brought with it lots of *evangelia*. These were announcements of good news for the people, like having the day off work, or off school. That was surely a good news announcement, an *evangelion*. So, at the heart of an *evangelion*, or a gospel, is good news, and people liked to receive many *evangelia*. They could not get enough of them.

However, when the Early Christians, such as Mark, started to use the word 'gospel', they used it in a singular sense and they did this to emphasize the fact that they were referring to one essential good news. This one good news was far superior to all the other numerous gospels of a lesser kind. Christians, just like the Jews, believed in one God and so there could only be one true gospel which told you the good news about that one true God. Thus Mark used the word 'gospel' in a singular sense only. So, he writes, right at the beginning of his gospel, 'The beginning of the good news of Jesus Christ the Son of God'.

Mark was so excited about this one 'Good News' that he just had to write it down for others to read. So for Mark the gospel was not just 'Good News' that should be proclaimed from the rooftops. Rather it was something so special that he had to write it down as well. What he did not know was that by writing it down he created a distinctive form of writing – the gospel.

Therefore, we have from Mark the first gospel about Jesus. Matthew, Luke and John who followed him were to write three more versions of that one 'Good News'. They each tell the 'Good News' about Jesus from a slightly different point of view.

So what is the 'Good News'?

The Early Christians were keen to spread the 'Good News' about Jesus. They called this the *Kerygma* or 'announcement'. The following statements became the main beliefs for the Christian Church:

◆ The Jews had been waiting for God to send a Messiah. This was to be a special person sent from God to be their leader. Early Christians believed that now the waiting was over. Jesus was indeed God's anointed one – the Messiah.

◆ The proof of this was that God raised Jesus from the dead.

◆ Because Jesus was the Messiah he would also judge the world at the end of time.

◆ Jesus showed through his example, his teaching and his miracles that everyone, not just the Jews, could be healed, forgiven and have a loving relationship with God their Father in Heaven.

◆ Because he rose from the dead Jesus showed his followers that death was not the end. They too could share in eternal life.

◆ Jesus promised his followers that they would receive God's Holy Spirit to be with them for ever. That promise was fulfilled at Pentecost when God's Spirit came as a great power.

◆ Early Christians believed that the Holy Spirit was now at work in the Church.

◆ Those who heard this 'Good News' about Jesus were taught that they should repent, change their lives and be baptized.

How does the Church express this 'Good News'?

These beliefs have always been at the heart of the teaching of missionaries and evangelists, but they could be summed up in a short simple statement of belief called 'The Creed' (derived from the Latin *credo* – 'I believe').

Two early creeds were quite simple – 'Jesus Christ is Lord' and 'I believe that Jesus Christ is the Son of God'.

Later on, however, longer creeds were written to express the essential beliefs of the Early Church. Thus the Apostles' Creed was written around CE 400. Nowadays there are a few different versions of the Creed used in worship. In a baptism service for example, the following version of the Creed is used. The statements of belief and 'Good News' are given by the congregation in response to questions from the Minister:

Minister	Do you believe and trust in God the Father?
All	**I believe in God, the Father almighty,** **creator of heaven and earth.**
Minister	Do you believe and trust in his Son Jesus Christ?
All	**I believe in Jesus Christ, his only Son, our Lord,** **who was conceived by the Holy Spirit,** **born of the Virgin Mary,** **suffered under Pontius Pilate,** **was crucified, died, and was buried;** **he descended to the dead.** **On the third day he rose again;** **he ascended into heaven,** **he is seated at the right hand of the Father,** **and he will come to judge the living and the dead.**
Minister	Do you believe and trust in the Holy Spirit?
All	**I believe in the Holy Spirit,** **the holy catholic Church,** **the communion of saints,** **the forgiveness of sins,** **the resurrection of the body,** **and the life everlasting.**
	Amen

Why were the gospels written?

Essentially because the gospel writers were so excited about their 'Good News' they wanted to share it with others. They wanted to help people to know about Jesus and why he was unique and special. They wanted people to realize that they too could have a loving Father in heaven, and that they too could have eternal life. As time passes memories fade and so it became very important to Christians in subsequent generations to know what actually happened and to have some teaching about what it all meant. Thus the gospel writers wrote it all down for all those who followed to hear the 'Good News' exactly as the gospel writers themselves had perceived it and to express what it meant to them.

Key ideas . . .
- The word 'gospel', derived from *evangelion*, means 'Good News'.
- Matthew, Mark, Luke and John each wrote a gospel.
- Early Christians spread the 'Good News'.
- They expressed this 'Good News' using creeds, which were statements of belief.

The Bible can help you . . .
- The four gospels can be found at the beginning of the New Testament.
- Some early simple Christian creeds can be found in Mark 8.29, 1 Corinthians 8.6, 1 Corinthians 12.3 and 1 Timothy 3.16.

Key words . . .
Gospel, *evangelion*, 'Good News', *kerygma*, Messiah, Holy Spirit, Church, creeds.

ACTIVITIES

1   Write your own creed to express what you think is the 'Good News' for Christians.

2   Write a statement of belief about yourself beginning 'I believe I am like my mother because . . .' or, 'I believe I am like my father because . . .' or 'I believe that I am not like my mother (or father) because . . .'.

3   Listen to a story as a group or watch an extract from a video. Now write the story without telling anyone else what you are writing. Share your story with a friend. Is it the same as someone else's? What have you included in your version that the others have missed out?

4   Write an individual account of a class event, e.g. sports day. Compare your accounts. Which one would you use to include in a school magazine and why? Consider the difficulties when choosing and the difficulties that the gospel writers would have encountered.

5   Write a biography of someone who is important to you.

6   Design a front cover for a New Testament to reflect the idea of 'Good News'.

Something to think about . . .

What was it about Jesus that made people want to write about his life?

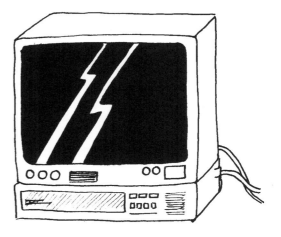

So, what are these four gospels?

Three of the gospels are quite similar. They are called the 'Synoptic Gospels' of Matthew, Mark and Luke. The fourth Gospel of John is rather different because it is more interested in the meaning of what Jesus did than in the events themselves.

The word 'synoptic' comes from 'synopsis' which means a general view or summary. These three gospels are remarkably alike in their general viewpoint and in their presentation of the events in Jesus' life.

Matthew's Gospel

It will help to know . . .

When was it written?

Although it is placed as the first of the four gospels in the New Testament, it is not thought by everyone to be the earliest gospel. It was probably written between CE 60 and CE 90.

Who wrote it?

Early second-century Christians claimed that the writer was Matthew whom Jesus called to be an apostle. However, many people believe that it was probably written by an unknown person who had been inspired by Matthew and who remembered a collection of Jesus' sayings that the apostle Matthew is said to have made.

What is special about it?

Some people call this gospel the 'Church's Gospel' because it is the only gospel that uses the word 'Church'. The Church is the vast community of disciples that Jesus called into being. Others call it 'The Jewish Gospel' because it shows a special interest in the concerns of the Early Christian Church as it emerged from its Jewish roots.

Although a Jew, Matthew showed his readers that they did not have to wait any longer for the long-expected Messiah. The Messiah had arrived and he was Jesus. So it is perhaps quite fitting that this gospel should be placed right at the beginning of the New Testament because it makes the link between the Old Testament (The Hebrew Bible) and the New Testament much more strongly than the other gospels do. The gospel writer is a teacher. He has written a gospel that has a clear and organized structure based on Jesus' teaching. The words of Jesus are mainly found in five great speeches:

- ◆ The Sermon on the Mount.
- ◆ Instructions to the disciples for their mission.
- ◆ Parables about the kingdom of heaven.
- ◆ What it means to be a disciple.
- ◆ Teaching about the coming of the kingdom of heaven.

Everything proceeds in an orderly fashion. The gospel starts with the birth, baptism and temptations of Jesus before going on to his ministry of preaching, teaching and healing. This happens in Galilee but after this Jesus journeys to Jerusalem. Here he is eventually crucified and his followers experience the resurrection. The gospel ends with Jesus' command to his disciples to go and make disciples of all the nations.

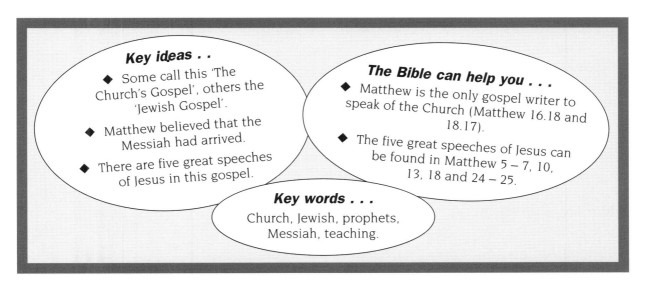

Key ideas · ·
- Some call this 'The Church's Gospel', others the 'Jewish Gospel'.
- Matthew believed that the Messiah had arrived.
- There are five great speeches of Jesus in this gospel.

The Bible can help you . . .
- Matthew is the only gospel writer to speak of the Church (Matthew 16.18 and 18.17).
- The five great speeches of Jesus can be found in Matthew 5 – 7, 10, 13, 18 and 24 – 25.

Key words . . .
Church, Jewish, prophets, Messiah, teaching.

ACTIVITIES

Matthew was very keen to help people live a life according to the teachings of Jesus and so his gospel contains some important advice and instruction. Particularly famous is his Sermon on the Mount. This is found in Matthew 5 – 7.

1   Read the whole of Matthew 6 to get a feel for the broad sweep of Jesus' teaching. Then choose one of the following sections and think about the questions:

Matthew 6.5-15 (*Advice on prayer*)	**Matthew 6.25-34** (*Advice on trusting God*)
◆ Where and when do you think it would be easiest to pray? ◆ Are lots of clever words needed for Christians to pray? ◆ How does the Lord's Prayer (Matthew 6.9-15) differ from the versions used today? ◆ Do you like the differences? Would you like to add anything? ◆ Do you find it easy to forgive your friends when they do something wrong to you?	◆ Are you anxious about the future? ◆ Jesus said 'Look at the birds' and 'Consider the lilies'. What are the bits of nature that you think would help Christians to praise God for his creation and loving care? ◆ Many people in our world are anxious about what they might have to eat or drink tomorrow. How do Christians show God's loving care and provision to them? ◆ Read Matthew 6.33 again. Find the words of the hymn 'Seek ye first the kingdom of God' in a hymn-book and read them carefully. What do you think Jesus meant by 'the kingdom of God'?

2   Read Matthew 5.2-12. Here Jesus gives the disciples a series of statements that would have turned some traditional views of the time on their heads. Christians call these statements 'the beatitudes' (coming from the Latin word *beati* meaning 'happy').

Choose one of these beatitudes and design a poster to reflect its meaning.

Or write a booklet explaining the beatitudes for a young child.

Or collect and look at newspaper cuttings. Do you think the teaching of the beatitudes is still relevant today? Why? As a group construct a montage of newspaper cuttings to reflect one beatitude.

3   Read Matthew 28.19-20 which speaks of Jesus sending his disciples out to spread the 'Good News' to others.

Imagine you are a modern-day apostle who feels God is calling you to spread the 'Good News' to others. Starting from your own home village/town construct an itinerary listing the places you plan to visit.

◆   Why have you chosen these places?

◆   What will you take with you?

◆   How would you travel?

◆   Would you raise funds in advance or would you plan to work to raise funds on route?

◆   List five aspects of the 'Good News' that you would want to share.

Something to think about . . .

Imagine a group of starving children in a famine-stricken country. Now complete the sentence 'Blessed are the . . .'

Mark's Gospel

It will help to know . . .

When was it written?

This is almost certainly the earliest of the gospels to be written and many people think it was written sometime before Jerusalem was destroyed by the Romans in CE 70, probably between CE 60 and CE 70.

Who wrote it?

Many people think that the gospel was written by John Mark, a Jewish disciple who is mentioned in Acts (12.12 and 15.37). His mother was Mary and their house became one of the earliest meeting places for Christians. Some also

think that this might have been the same young man mentioned in 14.51, 52 of Mark's Gospel who ran away naked when Jesus was arrested in the garden of Gethsemane the night before he died. It is believed that the gospel was written in Rome and that Mark got a lot of his stories from Peter the apostle who spent so much time with Jesus.

What is special about it?

Mark's Gospel is an exciting one to read. It is short, fast moving and action packed. Whereas Matthew shows Jesus to be a great teacher, Mark shows Jesus as a man of action. He is 'immediately' seen to be doing things. Indeed the word 'immediately' appears about 40 times in this gospel in the *New Revised Standard Version* of the Bible. This gospel recalls clear evidence of eyewitness reporting. Like Matthew, Mark attempts to persuade the Jews that Jesus is indeed the Messiah.

Key ideas . . .

◆ The gospel is fast moving.

◆ Jesus is named as the Son of God.

◆ Jesus is a great teacher and a man of action.

The Bible can help you . . .

◆ Above all Mark wanted to convince his readers that Jesus was indeed the Son of God (Mark 1.1 and 11, 5.7, 9.7, 14.61-62, 15.39). He does this by describing miraculous things done by Jesus. For those who had eyes to see, these mighty acts were signs of the presence of God's power and signs that Jesus had to be the Son of God. So, what is the sequence of this action-packed gospel?

◆ Mark 1.1-13: the beginning of Jesus' public life (with John the Baptist paving the way, Jesus' baptism, and Jesus' temptation).

◆ Mark 1.14 – 9.50: a fast-moving account of Jesus' preaching, teaching and healing in Galilee.

◆ Mark 10: a turning point. Jesus journeys to Jerusalem to suffering and to death.

◆ Mark 11 – 15. The last week of Jesus' life ending with his Crucifixion and burial.

◆ The Resurrection.

Key words . . .

Action, 'immediately', Son of God, miracles.

ACTIVITIES

Something to think about . . .

If you had 'good news' to tell the world today, how would you do it?

1   Read Mark 16.1-8. It is worth noting that the earliest copies of Mark's Gospel ended abruptly at 16.8 with the women running away from the empty tomb.

Now think about the following questions:

◆ Why do you think that Mark did not need to say any more?

◆ If this gospel originally ended at 16.8 why do you think someone later added the extra verses (9-20)?

◆ Read Mark 16.9-20 carefully. What differences do these verses make to the ending of the gospel?

2   Read the account of Jesus calling his disciples (Mark 1.16-20). Now imagine that Jesus is going to arrive in twenty minutes to visit you.

In a group, 'brainstorm':

◆ How you might react.

◆ What would your feelings be?

◆ What questions would you want to ask him?

◆ What do you think Jesus would say to you?

◆ Consider whether or not you would be prepared to leave everything to go with him. Would you worry about what other people thought about you and your response?

3   If you could write an alternative ending to Mark's Gospel what would you include?

Luke's Gospel

It will help to know . . .

When was it written?

The gospel is believed to have been written towards the end of the first century, i.e. sometime between CE 60 and CE 85.

Who wrote it?

From quite early on the author of this gospel was believed to be Luke, a non-Jewish (Gentile) doctor who travelled with the apostle Paul on many of his journeys. He is also believed to have written the Book of Acts which follows the gospels in the New Testament. He was Greek-speaking.

What is special about it?

The gospel was mainly written for non-Jewish people (the so-called Gentiles) to reassure them that whilst Jesus came first of all to the Jews the 'Good News' was for everyone – for the whole world. Luke gives this reassurance by explaining:

◆ Jesus' family tree could be traced right back to Adam, the father of the whole human race, not just to Abraham, the father of the Jews. (See Luke 3.23-38 and compare with Matthew 1.1-16. Can you see the difference?).

◆ Luke includes references that affirm the Samaritan people even though Jews despised them. (see Luke 10.30-37, 17.11-19)

◆ Luke indicates that women have an important place amongst the followers of Jesus (see Luke 7.36-50, 8.1-3 and 10.38-42). Remember that for Jews at the time of Jesus women had a subservient role.

◆ Luke makes it clear that the Gentiles would have the chance to hear the 'Good News' about Jesus and a chance to respond to it (Luke 2.32, 3.6, 24.47).

Key ideas . . .
◆ Written for non-Jewish people (the Gentiles).
◆ 'Good News' is for all people.

The Bible can help you . . .
Luke's Gospel can be divided into five main sections:
◆ Luke 1.1 – 4.13: the births of John the Baptist and Jesus, Jesus as a boy in the Temple, the ministry of John the Baptist, the baptism, genealogy and temptations of Jesus.
◆ Luke 4.14 – 9.50: Jesus in Galilee teaching, healing, calling the disciples.
◆ Luke 9.51 – 19.27: Jesus on the way to Jerusalem with more teaching and, in particular, with more parables.
◆ Luke 19.28 – 23.56: Jesus in Jerusalem, in the temple, in disputes, more teaching, the last supper and his betrayal, his arrest, trial, Crucifixion and burial.
◆ Luke 24: Jesus is raised from the dead.
◆ Luke writes many unique and very special stories such as the Good Samaritan (Luke 10.25-37) and the Prodigal Son (Luke 15.11-32).

Key words . . .
Gentile doctor, gospel for all, key stories.

ACTIVITIES

1 Read the Good Samaritan story (Luke 10.25-37). Think about the following questions:

◆ Why do you think Luke included the story in his gospel?

◆ What do the stories tell you about God and what he expects?

◆ Which character in the story do you most feel like? Why?

◆ Write or act out a modern-day version of the story.

2 Read the story of the Prodigal Son (Luke 15.11-32)

Write out the conversation that could have taken place between:

a) The father and the elder son *and*

b) The two brothers.

Alternatively write the letter that the younger brother might have written to his father to say why he wanted to come home.

3 Read the story of the healing of the ten lepers (Luke 17.11-19), then:

◆ Imagine you are being isolated from everyone because of an illness. How do you feel? What would you miss?

◆ Imagine you are suddenly healed from this illness. How would you react?

◆ Imagine you are one of the ten healed lepers. Would you be like the men who just ran off or like the one who remembered to thank Jesus?

Now write an interview with:

a) A leper who ran away without giving thanks.

b) The leper who returned to thank Jesus.

Pay particular attention to the feelings of the two both before and after the healing. Ask them also how the healing would change their lives.

Something to think about . . .
In Jesus' day leprosy was a disease that isolated people because no one wanted to touch them or be with them. Which illnesses of the body or the mind isolate people today?

John's Gospel

It will help to know . . .

When was it written?

It is not certain when this gospel was written. For a long time it was believed it was written between CE 90 and CE 100, but some people now believe it could have been written earlier, maybe as early as CE 60.

Who wrote it?

The writer of this gospel has long been held to be 'the disciple whom Jesus loved', that is John the Apostle, the son of Zebedee. It could, though, have been written by a follower of John who listened carefully to everything John had told him. Later he was thought to have taken Mary the mother of Jesus to Ephesus where he died at a ripe old age.

What is special about it?

As John was a Jew, he uses many Jewish themes from the Old Testament. This gospel is very different from the other three. The differences are partly in the setting: the other three gospels are mainly set in Galilee but John's is mainly set in Jerusalem. More important though is the difference in style. It is true that just like the other gospel writers John is concerned with the person of Jesus and with real events, but he succeeds in getting beyond these and working out their meaning. Thus John wants to explain the mystery of the person of Jesus. So he describes Jesus as always having been present, even when God was creating the world. Likewise he is presented as being a man yet showing us something of the nature of God (John 1.14, 18).

John uses symbols from everyday life to help us understand the significance of Jesus' life, symbols such as shepherds, doors, bread, water, light, life. A favourite word of his was 'love'. This gospel is both gripping and mysterious.

What are miracles?

Some of the most dramatic stories told about Jesus by John are those which describe him performing miracles. These miracles range from healing people to bringing the dead back to life. In the other gospels these miracles are described as 'mighty works' because they were believed to be done through the power of God. They are also called 'wonders' because those who saw them were amazed.

John prefers to call them 'signs', because just as signposts show you the way to a destination, so the miracles were believed by those who saw or heard of them to point to a belief that Jesus was not just an ordinary human being but that he was divine.

But what is a miracle? Dictionaries define a miracle as an event that appears inexplicable by the laws of nature and so is held to be 'supernatural' in nature, or an 'act of God'.

Miracles are certainly not magic. Although magic is dramatic and at first you just can't believe it because it seems impossible, all magic can ultimately be explained. Miracles by definition are inexplicable. Many people question the possibility of miracles and this has to be expected. Some don't believe they can happen because they have never seen or experienced one. To others miracles seem 'unscientific' and therefore couldn't possibly happen. For Christians these questions are still important, but because of their belief in God and their faith in Jesus they accept the miracles as 'mighty works', 'wonders' and 'signs'. After all, if God could create the world out of nothing, miracles must surely be possible. Indeed Jesus said 'What is impossible for man is possible for God.' (Luke 18.27)

For Christians the most important display of God's power, his greatest miracle, was the Resurrection of Jesus from the dead.

The Bible can help you . . .
There are six main sections to the gospel:

◆ John includes a prologue which presents Jesus as the Word of God. This may sound complicated, but it will be explained later in this book (see p. 36).

◆ John 2 – 11.57: a section sometimes called the 'book of signs'. There are signs to point readers towards believing that Jesus really is the Messiah, the Son of God (John 20.31). These signs are miracles.

◆ John 12: the anointing of Jesus and his dramatic entry into Jerusalem.

◆ John 13 – 17 describes Jesus' fellowship with his followers and includes the accounts of the events in the upper room and garden of Gethsemane shortly before his arrest.

◆ John 18 and 19 cover the arrest, trial, Crucifixion, and burial of Jesus.

◆ John 20 – 21 describe everything related to Jesus rising from death including the empty tomb, Jesus appearing to Mary Magdalene, Jesus meeting with Thomas, Jesus and his disciples at the lakeside.

Key ideas . . .
◆ Mainly set in Jerusalem.
◆ Concerned with real events but also with the meaning of it all.
◆ Explains the mystery of Jesus.
◆ For Christians, John reveals the true nature of God.

Key words . . .
Meaning, mystery, creation, signs, symbols, Father, love.

ACTIVITIES

In John 2.1-11 we find the account of the wedding at Cana of Galilee, when Jesus changed water into wine. At the end of this miracle John writes that this is the first sign that Jesus did and that it 'revealed his glory; and his disciples believed in him'. This is just one of the seven such signs in John 2 – 11 and these signs were deliberately included to lead people into believing that Jesus was the Son of God.

The other six signs are:

◆ healing an official's son (John 4.46-54)

◆ healing at the pool of Bethesda (John 5.1-9)

- ◆ feeding of the 5,000 (John 6.1-15)

- ◆ walking on water (John 6.16-21)

- ◆ healing a man born blind (John 9)

- ◆ raising Lazarus from the dead (John 11.1-44)

1 Read the account of the feeding of the 5,000 (John 6.1-15). Think about the following questions:

- ◆ Why were so many people following Jesus?

- ◆ What do you think is the significance of there being so much food left over (12 baskets full)?

- ◆ Do you think that people who read about this 'sign' would have been led to a similar belief? (read John 20.30-31)

- ◆ Imagine that you were the boy in the story. Write the entry that you might have made in your diary for that day.

2 The story of the feeding of the 5,000 is found in every gospel but each account is slightly different. Read the account in Matthew's Gospel (14.13-21) and compare it with this account in John 6.1-15. How do the stories differ?

Something to think about . . .

Do you see evidence of miracles today?

3 Read the account of the healing of a man born blind (John 9.1-12). Imagine you are a reporter from a local newspaper. Write an account of the interview you held with the man after his sight was restored. What happened? How did he feel? How did the people react?

4 Design a stained-glass window to illustrate one of the seven signs (miracles).

A journey through the Church past and present

The birth of the Christian Church

It will help to know . . .

The Feast of Pentecost

On the day of Pentecost the disciples were gathered in the upper room of a house in Jerusalem and had an extraordinary experience. As a result, later Christians came to see this day as the birthday of the Church.

On that day Jerusalem was crowded with people who had travelled from all over the world. They had come to celebrate the feast of Shavuot, an important time when Jews remember that God has given them a very special gift. This gift was the Ten Commandments written on stones and given to Moses on the top of Mount Sinai. Such was the importance of this festival to Jews that they came from all over the world as pilgrims to share in the great day. No wonder Jerusalem was crowded that day. So what happened to the disciples gathered in an upper room?

The Holy Spirit comes

The following events of Pentecost are described in the Acts of the Apostles. It is recalled that as the disciples were gathered together the Spirit of God came upon them. Jews had always believed in the spirit. The Jews saw God's Spirit as being his power at work in the world, in creation, in giving life and in inspiring people. Now the disciples experienced the coming of God's Spirit 'like a rushing mighty wind' and with fire. This may seem strange to us but the Jews would have understood it more easily. There are many references to the Spirit and the work of the Spirit in the Old Testament. In the Old Testament fire and wind were signs to show that God was really present (see also p. 53). It was a way by which they could understand that God was with them in great power. Naturally the disciples were filled with joy.

All the people outside wanted to know what was going on so they all gathered around. To their amazement the disciples started to speak in different languages. Everyone understood the disciples clearly. It really did not matter what part of the world they came from. The Acts of the Apostles says that it included Jews from Parthia, Media, Elam and Mesopotamia, all of which are lands outside the Roman Empire. But as if that was not enough, there follows a list of provinces from within the Roman Empire, provinces like Cappadocia, Pontus, Asia, Phrygia and Pamphylia. Jews had come from those places as well as from Egypt, from Cyrene in North Africa, from Rome, from Crete, and from Arabia. This meant that on that one day the 'Good News' was heard by Jews who had come from all lands between Italy in the west and almost the borders of India in the east. They all heard the disciples speak in their own languages. No wonder they were amazed.

Because the disciples were so excited many in the crowd thought they were drunk. Peter explained to the crowd that they were quite sober, it was just that they were filled with the Holy Spirit as the prophet Joel in the Old Testament had promised. This is what Joel said: 'God says, I will pour out my spirit on all flesh'. Now the disciples believed it was happening.

New believers

There was great excitement and many wanted to know more about what was happening. Peter stood up and told them all the 'Good News'. He explained carefully what had happened and how they too could have that new special relationship with God through the Holy Spirit. Many wanted to know how and so Peter told them that all they had to do was to be sorry for all the things they had done wrong, believe in Jesus and be baptized. Then he assured them that they would experience the power and energy of the Holy Spirit.

The New Testament tells how on that that day 3,000 people became believers in Jesus and were baptized. It must have been a dramatic sight. As a consequence Christians say that the day of Pentecost was the birthday of the Christian Church and it has been kept as a festival of the Holy Spirit ever since.

When they went back to their countries these new Christians would have been able to tell all their friends all about Jesus and about being filled with the Holy Spirit. The Christian Church was beginning to spread.

Key ideas . . .
- Disciples gathered in Jerusalem for the Jewish feast of Shavuot.
- The coming of the Holy Spirit was described to be like a rushing wind and fire.
- The disciples spoke in languages that everybody could understand.
- 3,000 people became believers. The Church was born.

The Bible can help you . . .
- The account of the Holy Spirit coming to the disciples can be found in Acts 2.1-4.
- You can read about the disciples speaking in other languages in Acts 2.5-13.
- Peter's teaching can be found in Acts 2.14-41.
- Joel's prophecy can also be found in Joel 2.28-32.

Key words . . .
Disciples, Pentecost, Holy Spirit, wind, fire, languages, Peter's teaching, new believers, birth of the Church

ACTIVITIES

1   Write a dialogue that could have taken place between two of the disciples in the upper room following the events of Pentecost. Say what they intend to do next.

2   Read Acts 2.5-12. Using a modern-day atlas or the Internet try to find out the names and locations of these places today.

3   Imagine that you have travelled from Egypt for the Jewish festival of Shavuot. Following the events that took place on the first Pentecost you were baptized and became a Christian. Design a postcard to send home using symbols of the Holy Spirit. Write on the card about your experience that day.

4   Find out all you can about the Jewish festival of Shavuot. Prepare a talk on this festival for another class.

Something to think about . . .

Can you think of a time when you got so excited about something that you just had to rush out and tell someone about it?
Did they listen?

Life in the Early Church

It will help to know . . .

The Church at Jerusalem

The first Christians continued to practise Jewish customs and to worship in the synagogues and in the temple, but they also enjoyed a close fellowship together. They met in each other's houses and shared a common meal called the *agape* (love feast). This was a symbol of their

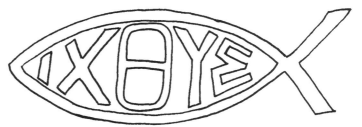

new-found love for each other within the Christian family. They also shared bread and wine together as Jesus had asked his followers to do at his Last Supper. As they did this they remembered him and felt his presence with them.

These Early Christians also shared their possessions with one another as a sign of their loving fellowship. Everything was put into a common pool for the leaders to share out according to need. This sharing was done freely, inspired by love.

Meanwhile the disciples were continuing to spread the 'Good News'. People started to call them apostles instead of disciples because, in addition to being just followers of Jesus, they were sent out with a job to do. They were ambassadors. Later on the apostles came to be known not only as people 'who were sent', but also as people who had witnessed the risen Christ.

The persecution and developments elsewhere

We must not, however, paint too rosy a picture of these Early Christian communities. It is true that the apostles grew popular through their teaching and preaching, but the Jewish authorities were becoming more and more suspicious of them. As a consequence the Christians were being persecuted. Stephen was stoned to death, becoming their first martyr. Many Christians were threatened, including Peter and John, but they refused to keep silent.

As a result of this persecution the believers scattered all over Judaea and Samaria, founding new Christian communities wherever they settled.

Meanwhile (around CE 34) there were important events developing elsewhere involving firstly a Pharisee called Saul and then Peter the Apostle.

Saul's conversion and the adventures of Paul

Saul had been brought up in Tarsus (in what is now Turkey). He was an educated Jew but also a Roman citizen. He was a tent-maker by profession and could speak Hebrew, Latin and Greek. He went to Jerusalem to train to become a rabbi. He was horrified at what the Christians were teaching for he was a very strict Jew. So he started to persecute them and had many of them thrown into prison, tortured or even killed. He wanted to nip this Christianity in the bud. One day he decided to go to Damascus to capture some of the Christians there, but the story describes how on the way he was blinded by a bright light and heard God speaking to him. It was an amazing, life-changing experience for Saul. Eventually his sight was restored; he became a Christian and was baptized. So Saul changed from being a persecutor of Christians to becoming an apostle himself and thereafter was called Paul. Paul was to have an important role in the growth and spread of the Christian Church.

Following his conversion Paul eventually made his way back to Jerusalem where he became friends with another Christian called Barnabas. They were to have many adventures together in later life. Paul became a powerful preacher and quickly made enemies amongst fanatical Jews.

During the next fifteen years he was to work tirelessly for the Christian cause. He spent the rest of his life making amends for the early persecution. He had many adventures, travelled extensively and was often in danger. However, he had a clear strategy for building up the Christian Church. This included:

- setting up churches in key towns;
- appointing elders in each church;
- revisiting the churches to encourage them;
- keeping in touch with the churches by letter.

As a result of Paul's efforts, the Christian Church spread throughout the Mediterranean. Paul was eventually taken to Rome where he was finally put to death. According to tradition, being a Roman citizen he was beheaded, unlike non-citizens who could be crucified.

Peter's vision

Peter was also working tirelessly to spread the 'Good News'. He had a vision from God and as a result went to visit a Roman soldier named Cornelius. Peter started telling Cornelius all about Jesus. The story describes how as Cornelius and his whole family listened, they were filled with the Holy Spirit just as Peter and the other disciples had been on the day of Pentecost. Cornelius and his family were not Jews, so how could this be?

Peter and others had to learn a valuable lesson: that anyone who believed in Jesus was accepted by God and could receive his Holy Spirit. Paul and Peter argued about this but it was finally agreed that you did not have to be a Jew; anybody from any nation could become a Christian. Such people who were not Jews were called Gentiles. So Christianity was possible for all people wherever they lived throughout the world. It was now clear that Christianity could spread beyond Israel.

When the Book of Acts ends, there were churches in all the main centres of the Roman Empire and from there the gospel was spreading out to surrounding areas. Many people were preaching the gospel and helping the churches to grow.

If Pentecost represented the birth of the Church, by about CE 64 it had certainly become an active toddler!

Leaders in the Early Christian Church

Often the Christian fellowships would give money to the apostles to distribute to the needy, but this began to take up a lot of the apostles' time. So the apostles decided to get extra help and chose seven men to be deacons. These deacons had the task of organizing support for the needy so that the apostles could get on with other work. So, these first deacons were servants of the Church and when they had been chosen the apostles 'laid hands on them'. This was a way of giving the deacons the authority of the Church, an authority that Jesus had himself given to the apostles.

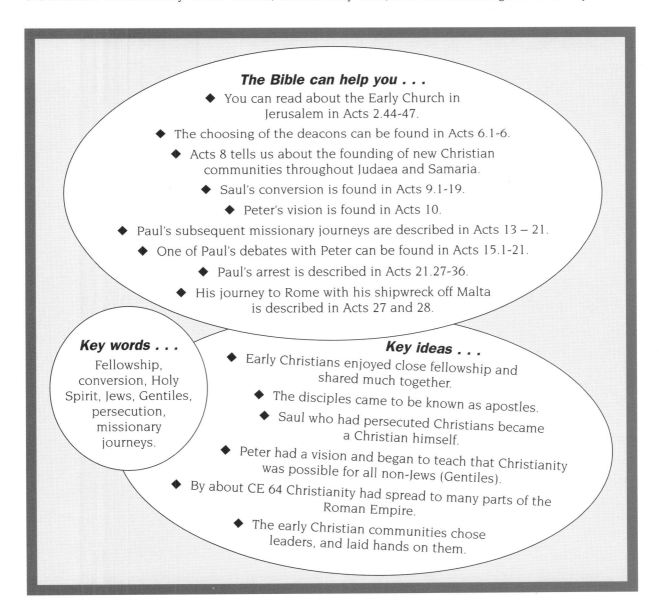

The Bible can help you . . .
- You can read about the Early Church in Jerusalem in Acts 2.44-47.
- The choosing of the deacons can be found in Acts 6.1-6.
- Acts 8 tells us about the founding of new Christian communities throughout Judaea and Samaria.
- Saul's conversion is found in Acts 9.1-19.
- Peter's vision is found in Acts 10.
- Paul's subsequent missionary journeys are described in Acts 13 – 21.
- One of Paul's debates with Peter can be found in Acts 15.1-21.
- Paul's arrest is described in Acts 21.27-36.
- His journey to Rome with his shipwreck off Malta is described in Acts 27 and 28.

Key words . . .
Fellowship, conversion, Holy Spirit, Jews, Gentiles, persecution, missionary journeys.

Key ideas . . .
- Early Christians enjoyed close fellowship and shared much together.
- The disciples came to be known as apostles.
- Saul who had persecuted Christians became a Christian himself.
- Peter had a vision and began to teach that Christianity was possible for all non-Jews (Gentiles).
- By about CE 64 Christianity had spread to many parts of the Roman Empire.
- The early Christian communities chose leaders, and laid hands on them.

ACTIVITIES

1   In small groups imagine you are a fellowship of Christians. Would you find it difficult to live your life in close fellowship, with others, just as those earliest Christians did in Acts 2.44-47? Write down a list of some difficulties that you might encounter, for example:

   ◆   What things would you find easy to share and what things would you find more difficult to share?

   ◆   Would you want leaders and how would you choose them?

   ◆   How would you authorize them to do their work?

   ◆   How would you keep contact with other Christians and how would you know you all believed the same things?

2   Find out about Peter's vision from Acts 10 and 11. Imagine you are Peter. Explain to the other disciples your reasons for ordering Cornelius and his family to be baptized (after all, they were Gentiles not Jews).

3   Find out more about Paul. There are many stories about his life. Design a board game to show some of the adventures in Paul's life.

4   Read either Acts 13.4-12 (Paul's visit to Cyprus) or Acts 14.6-20 (Paul's visit to Lystra).

   Imagine you are a BBC news reporter and you have to send a report back to England about what happened when Paul arrived in your chosen location. What was his message? What did he do? How did the crowd react?

Something to think about . . .

What was it about Jesus that inspired the apostles to leave their homes, jobs and loved ones in order to spread the 'Good News'?

The growth of the Church

It will help to know . . .

Influence of Constantine

For almost three centuries after the death of Christ the Christian Church faced persecution. Christians needed to be very brave and many became martyrs for their faith. All this persecution largely came to an end though after CE 311 when Constantine became the new Roman Emperor. His mother Helen was a Christian. Christians were no longer called traitors for refusing to believe that the Roman Emperor was a god. In CE 313 a law called 'the Edict of Milan' was passed and this allowed people to be Christians. So for the first time it was legal within the Roman law to be a Christian and openly to practise Christian belief without fear of persecution. To help them Constantine called a great council of all the church leaders in a place called Nicaea, with the task of drawing up a list of what Christians believe. This list was called the Nicene Creed and is still used in the Church today. The toleration of Christianity under Constantine produced some immediate changes. He ordered that Sunday was to be a public holiday. This made it easier for people to go to meet for worship and so congregations grew. Christian festivals tended to multiply and pilgrimages to the Holy Land became common and many Churches were erected so the Church began to spread and grow.

Eastern Orthodox Church

Rome had always been the capital of the Roman Empire but in CE 330 Emperor Constantine decided to create a new capital city called Constantinople (which is now called Istanbul). This Christian city was on a busy trading route near the Bosphorus in Turkey. This was right in the middle of the Roman Empire where Europe and Asia meet.

The main church in the city was the Church of the Holy Wisdom: no image of Roman or Greek gods was allowed. The Bishop of Constantinople was equal to the Bishop of Rome and so was very important. However, this created two main centres of Christianity – in the West (centred on Rome) and in the East (centred on Constantinople). Communication was not good and different practices developed between the two Churches (for example the way they celebrated their Holy Communion). They also disagreed as to who the real leader of the Church was, and on the precise wording of their creeds. This resulted in division. The Eastern Church came to be known as the Eastern Orthodox Church and over the centuries 15 separate branches of the Eastern Orthodox Church developed (mainly in Eastern Mediterranean countries, including Egypt, and in Russia). Each of these Churches was ruled by a patriarch, but the Patriarch of Constantinople was considered to be their overall leader. Of these Orthodox Churches, the one in Russia was established by Basil in CE 988. There are currently some 70 million baptized Orthodox Christians in Russia.

The Greek Orthodox Church, however, still remains one of the strongest of the Orthodox Churches, not only in Greece but throughout the world where those who have left Greece have established Orthodox Churches in their new countries.

The split between East and West

An important split between the Western and Eastern Churches came in 1054 when the Bishop of Rome (the Pope) and the Bishop of Constantinople fell out over how the Church should be governed. From then on the Churches went their different ways. The leader of the Western Church was the Pope and he is still the leader of the Roman Catholic Church. The leader of the Eastern Church is the Patriarch of Constantinople.

Orthodox churches remained very colourful, with beautiful paintings about the life of Jesus painted on the walls. These are called frescos. Many churches also contained icons – pictures of Jesus or the saints. These are kissed as people enter the church.

The Western (Roman Catholic) Church

The Bishop of Rome (the Pope) became very influential and Emperor Constantine gave much land to the Pope. The Western Church thus became stronger and more powerful.

During the 400 years after Constantine, people from Gibraltar to the Baltic were converted to Christianity, changing the face of the Christian Church. Often they were converted by passing on the faith from one tribe to another, sometimes by missionary saints. So Christianity spread, but the driving force was still the Roman Empire where to be civilized and educated was also to be Christian.

Christianity arrived in Britain with the Romans. The first Briton to die for his Christian beliefs was St Alban in about CE 250. However, when Britain was invaded nearly 200 years later by the Angles and Saxons from northern Europe, the Christian Britons retreated into Wales and Cornwall and the rest of England became a pagan country once again.

In CE 432 St Patrick, a Briton who was also a Roman citizen, sailed to Ireland to convert the Irish. Later in CE 563, St Columba took Christianity to Iona in the Western Isles of Scotland. As the monastic community on Iona grew, so too did Iona as a centre of Christianity. Gradually Christianity became more widespread and in CE 634 St Aidan took it to the rest of Scotland and to northern England. This enabled the Christian gospel to spread south and throughout Britain.

During this period, the Pope sent a group of Benedictine monks to England from Rome in order to reintroduce the gospel to the south of England. In CE 597 St Augustine founded the Cathedral Church in Canterbury and became Bishop there. One of his companions, St Paulinus travelled north and became the first Bishop of York. Thus Christianity had gone full circle from the south of England to Wales, Ireland, Scotland and back through England. Britain had become a Christian nation and adopted the Roman Catholic faith with the Pope as its head.

During the Middle Ages Christianity became widespread throughout the land. The language of the Roman Catholic Church was Latin, simply because that was the language used by educated people in the West. It continued to be the main language used in services right up to 1965. Nowadays most services are in the local language (the vernacular).

Early Bibles and most of the early official documents were also written in Latin. The advantage of this one universal language was that the services were the same throughout the Romanic world. It did mean, however, that only educated people could fully understand what was being said. Books were very expensive and had to be copied carefully by hand.

Monks and monasteries

As in the early Christian Church, there were bishops, priests and deacons now serving throughout the world. Some of these clergy, as they were called, were also monks. The monks lived in monasteries living a life of prayer and devotion, but also having an important role in copying the Bible.

Jerome re-translated the texts from Greek and Hebrew into Latin. He had searched for the origins of the scriptures and he even travelled to Bethlehem in CE 386 to revise the books of the Hebrew Bible that Christians now call the Old Testament. Monks became renowned for study and for their teaching skills. However, they also looked after the sick and the poor, and provided accommodation for weary travellers, especially pilgrims.

Monasticism had already taken root in the Eastern Church by the time Martin of Tours became the first well-known monk in the Western Church. He lived in France and died in CE 397.

In the years that followed, monasteries were established throughout the world, both in the East and in the West. By the late fifth century, for example, monasteries had already taken root in Ireland. These monasteries all had their practices, rules and customs, but from the later sixth century it was the rule of Benedict that took over from most other Western monastic rules. The rule was based on two activities: prayer and work. The 'Benedictine' monks, as they were called, did much to keep up spiritual standards during subsequent centuries when monasticism flourished. Some other rules for monks emerged in the Church of the time including those for Cistercians (1098), the Dominicans (1220) and the Franciscans (1210). They differed really on the balance between work, study, prayer and devotion to poverty.

Key ideas . . .
◆ Early Christians faced immense persecution.
◆ Emperor Constantine made Christianity lawful and creeds were drawn up.
◆ The Church spread throughout the Roman Empire.
◆ Constantinople became the centre of the Eastern Orthodox Church.
◆ Rome became the centre of the Western Roman Catholic Church.
◆ Orthodox Churches became renowned for their icons.
◆ The Eastern and Western Churches became separated.
◆ Christianity arrived in Britain.
◆ Monasticism flourished.

Key words . . .
Persecution, Constantine, Nicene Creed, Eastern Orthodox, Roman Catholic, schism, Pope, patriarch, icons, monasticism.

The Bible can help you . . .
◆ Accounts of the persecution of early Christians can be found in Acts 5.17-42, Acts 7.54-60 and Acts 8.1-3. Paul's (Saul's) admission to being involved in persecuting the Christians is found in many places including Acts 26.11, Galatians 1.23 and 4.29.

ACTIVITIES

1   Find out about icons and their use in the Orthodox tradition today.

2   Design and paint either a fresco representing a stage in the life of Jesus or an icon of your favourite saint.

3   Visit your local Roman Catholic Church and find out more about their beliefs, practices, the role of the Pope and why Roman Catholics reserve a special place in their devotions for Mary the Mother of Jesus.

4   Roman Catholics often use a rosary to help them to pray. This is like a necklace of beads with a crucifix (a cross with a figure of Jesus on it). It is used to help the person focus on the Creed, the Lord's Prayer and the special prayers to Mary. Obtain a rosary and speculate on its use. Then:

Either invite a Roman Catholic to explain how it is used as a help in praying. Get him/her to tell you the 'Hail Mary' prayer and write it down. Write and illustrate a simple explanation of the use of the rosary. Make a drawing of the rosary indicating what prayers might be said in each section.

Or read the two stories from the Bible which are associated with the saying of the rosary. These are the annunciation to Mary (Luke 1.26-38) and Mary's visitation to Elizabeth (Luke 1.39-45). Now write a series of prayers of thanks for the annunciation and visitation that a Christian could use for prayer as they work around the rosary.

5   Find out more about the spread of Christianity in Britain. Write a class book about the Early Christian saints in Britain (for example Alban, Patrick, Augustine, Columba).

6   Monks were often very artistic in their copying of manuscripts and the 'illuminated' letters they produced were often used as a form of prayer and meditation. The following picture illustrates an 'illuminated' letter 'T' from the Book of Kells.

This letter 'T' is a beast complete with head, neck, body, tail, two forelegs and two hind legs. The other contents are four reptiles with heads, bodies and tails.

Research the use of illuminated letters in Early Christian manuscripts. Now find the opening sentence to your favourite Bible story and write this out using the technique employed by the monks.

Something to think about . . .

What do you think it would be like if we did not have any books?

The Reformation – the birth of the Anglican Church

It will help to know . . .

The Reformation was a popular movement in Northern Europe at the beginning of the sixteenth century which eventually led to the formation of different branches of the Church we see today (we call them 'denominations'). It was a movement by people who were disillusioned with the Roman Catholic Church because they felt it was not paying enough attention to the Bible, that it was making Christian belief too complicated, and that many of the Church leaders were becoming too relaxed about moral corruption.

Protestants

The movement gained momentum when in 1517 a priest called Martin Luther in eastern Germany demanded that the Roman Catholic Church address such issues. When he didn't get the response he wanted he reluctantly formed a breakaway church which came to be known as the Lutheran Church. All those who broke away from the Catholic Church came to be known as Protestants (simply because they were protesting against the Roman Catholic Church).

The other major centre for the Reformation on the continent was Geneva in Switzerland where John Calvin formed a breakaway church in 1541. His movement subsequently embraced France as well, and also influenced Scotland because one of Calvin's admirers, a man called John Knox, took Calvin's ideas back to the Church in Scotland.

The Church of England

In Europe politics as well as religion had a large influence on the Reformation. At the time of the Reformation Henry VIII was a devout Catholic. In fact he had been given the title 'Defender of the Faith'. However, in 1527 he decided to divorce his wife Catherine of Aragon. Henry had needed to produce a son and heir but felt that it was God's punishment upon him for marrying Catherine, his brother's widow, that she was unable to bear him a son (Leviticus 18.16). Pope Clement VII would not give him permission to divorce and the only way Henry could obtain one and marry again was to separate the Church in England from the authority of the Pope in Rome. Henry became head of the Church in England. Many supported him. Some who did not were beheaded and thus became martyrs because they were prepared to die for their faith. Thomas Cranmer was a leader of the religious movement in Britain against Rome and he was eventually made Archbishop of Canterbury. Henry knew that the monasteries were powerful and very supportive of the Pope. To remove their influence he had many of them destroyed. This ended a long period of influential monasticism.

After the short reign of Edward VI there was a brief period when England returned to the Roman Catholic faith under Mary Tudor. As a consequence Thomas Cranmer was forced to stand down as archbishop and was eventually executed (burnt at the stake) for refusing to give his allegiance to the Roman Catholic Church. Thus he also became a martyr. When Elizabeth I became queen in 1558 she restored the reformed Church in England. From that time the Church of England has been the official Church in England. Within this Church the creeds and many original practices have been retained.

After the Reformation the main change that ordinary parishioners experienced was that their services were in English, not Latin. Thomas Cranmer, the Archbishop of Canterbury at that time, had been given the task of producing a new prayer book in English. *The Book of Common Prayer* contains a number of statements known as the Thirty-Nine Articles which summarize the beliefs of the Church of England. It also contains the words of the services to be used in church. More recently the Church of England has authorized additional prayer books. These include *The Alternative Service Book* (1980; its period of authorization ended in 2000) and its successor *Common Worship* (2000).

Thus, for over 300 years the Church of England has been the national Church. Ever since the reign of Elizabeth I the monarch of England has been the official head of the Church of England. Even today it is the Queen and Prime Minister who decide who are appointed to the role of bishop in the Church of England, and any modification to the prayer books used has to be debated in parliament.

The Anglican Communion

In the nineteenth century, with the spread of the British Empire, the Church of England sent missionaries overseas to preach the message of Jesus Christ. As a consequence, the Church of England became represented in many more countries including Africa, the West Indies, Australia, New Zealand, India and parts of Asia. The association of churches is known as the Anglican Communion. The Anglican Church in each of these countries has an archbishop and bishops as in the Church of England. The Church of England is the 'Mother Church' of this Anglican Communion.

Other denominations

Over the course of time, not everybody in England was happy with the Church of England and so new Protestant groups split away from it. The following denominations broke away during the reign of Elizabeth I:

The Presbyterians disliked the leaders of each congregation being called 'priests'. They preferred to call them 'presbyters' since this was what they were called in the New Testament.

The Baptists disliked infant baptism because they did not think this was done in accordance with the New Testament and they did not believe that infants were able to make a commitment for themselves.

The Puritans disliked any form of worship that could not be found in the New Testament.

The Methodists About 200 years after the Reformation another group broke away from the Church of England. These were the Methodists who were led by John and Charles Wesley. They thought the Church of England had lost touch with God and also the people, and they wanted to restore the enthusiasm and spontaneity of the Church of the first century. They were called Methodists because they were so methodical in all they did. They became a separate Church in 1784, and spread throughout North America, the West Indies, Sri Lanka, India, China and Africa.

The Salvation Army A breakaway group from the Methodist Church was The Salvation Army which was founded in 1865 by William Booth. He felt that the Church wasn't doing enough to help poor people, so he set up centres where they could receive help. This began in London but is now worldwide and deeply respected for its work with the poor and needy.

Christians often feel it is sad that so many modern-day Christians belong to separate denominations. The modern-day ecumenical movement seeks to find ways to resolve the differences and form a sense of unity amongst all these different Churches.

Key ideas . . .

◆ Protestants protested against the Roman Catholic Church and broke away.

◆ The Reformation in England was tied up with politics but gave birth to the Church of England, which produced its own prayer books.

◆ Other denominations emerged.

◆ With the spread of the British Empire, the Anglican Communion was formed.

◆ There have been many followers of Jesus who would rather die than betray him or denounce their faith. Such martyrs have been revered by the Church.

Key words . . .

Reformation, separation, Lutherans, Protestants, Calvinists, Church of England, Cranmer, denominations, Anglican Communion, martyrs.

The Bible can help you . . .

◆ Many people are sad that the Christian Church is so divided. They refer to Jesus' desire that his flock be one people (John 10.16, 17.21).

ACTIVITIES

1   Obtain a copy of the 1662 *Book of Common Prayer* which Thomas Cranmer wrote and originally published in 1549 and 1552. (Your local Anglican church will lend you one.) Prior to 1662 services had been in Latin and a main aim for Cranmer was to make the services understandable to the people of his day.

    Read his introduction to the Marriage Service which begins, 'Dearly beloved, we are gathered together here in the sight of God . . .'

    Rewrite Cranmer's introduction in your own words changing anything that you think needs to be changed for society today.

2   Identify the location of churches on your local map. Find out which denomination these churches are. Choose two of them. Find out what services take place at these two churches. Invite the leader at each of these churches to visit your school to tell you what is different and special about their church. How do they differ from the Church of England?

3   Invite a representative of your local Salvation Army to visit your school. Ask him/her to bring along key artefacts (uniform, banner, motto, etc.) together with pictures/video of their meeting place.

    Ask him/her to talk about key features of their worship and ministry.

    Discuss differences and similarities between the Church of England and the Salvation Army. Look at images and symbols in both which remind Christians about Jesus and God. Make a Venn diagram to compare the two churches.

4   If Jesus returned, do you think he would find the church today appropriate for worship? Select one aspect from each denomination that he might like. Write down some of your ideas.

5   Throughout the history of Christianity there have been followers of Jesus who would rather die than betray him. These were called martyrs and they have always been held in high regard by the Church. At the time of the Early Church Christians were constantly hounded and persecuted. Many died for their faith. The historian Tacitus wrote that in CE 64 Emperor Nero 'charged and tortured some people hated for their evil practice, the group popularly known as Christians'. They were arrested. Tacitus reports: 'in their deaths they were made a mockery. They were covered in the skins of wild animals, torn to death by dogs, crucified or set on fire, so that when darkness fell they burned like torches in the night.'

Unfortunately such persecution, death and martyrdom were not confined to the Early Church; they have continued down the centuries. The list is extensive but includes such well-known martyrs as Stephen (Acts 6 – 7), Thomas Becket, Thomas Cranmer, Thomas More, Joan of Arc. Using your library resources and the Internet discover what you can about two such martyrs. What did they die for?

6   Discover what you can about the life of a recent martyr such as Martin Luther King. What did he or she die for? Do you consider them to be true martyrs? Give your reasons.

Something to think about . . .

Can you think of anything that you feel so strongly about that you would be prepared to die for it?

A journey through the Church year

Introduction

The following words are taken from the Victorian children's hymn written by A. C. Hankey (1834–1911). They were used to help children remember the seasons of the Church year. Just as the seasons of the calendar year begin with spring and end with winter, so the Church year begins with Advent and ends with the Feast of Christ the King on the Sunday before the following Advent. In between we find Christmas, Epiphany, Lent, Easter, Ascension, Pentecost and Trinity.

> Advent tells us Christ is near:
> Christmas tells us Christ is here!
> In Epiphany we trace
> All the glory of his grace.
>
> Those three Sundays before Lent
> Will prepare us to repent;
> That in Lent we may begin
> Earnestly to mourn for sin.
>
> Holy Week and Easter, then,
> Tell who died and rose again:
> O that happy Easter day!
> 'Christ is risen indeed,' we say.
>
> Yes and Christ ascended too,
> To prepare a place for you;
> So we give him special praise,
> After those great forty days.
>
> Then he sent the Holy Ghost,
> On the Day of Pentecost,
> With us ever to abide:
> Well may we keep Whitsuntide!
>
> Last of all we humbly sing
> Glory to our God and King,
> Glory to the One in Three
> On the feast of Trinity.

In this chapter we shall journey through the Church year beginning with Advent, Christmas and Epiphany. We shall also explore the different liturgical colours used by some Christian denominations to celebrate these seasons although it is worth noting that local custom does vary.

Advent

It will help to know . . .

Advent begins on the Sunday nearest to 30 November and takes its name from the Latin word *venere* which means 'to come'. It is usually regarded as a time of reflection and penitence in preparation for Christmas. The predominant theme is one of hope linked to the 'coming of the kingdom' (see also p. 6). Many churches and individual Christian families now mark this season with an Advent calendar or wreath like the one below.

The first candle is lit on Advent Sunday and then an additional one is lit on each of the following Sundays until finally the central candle is lit on Christmas Day. The central candle symbolizes Jesus as the light of the world. The current themes of the candles and Sundays in Advent are as follows:

1   The Patriarchs

2   The prophets

3   John the Baptist

4   The Blessed Virgin Mary

5   The Nativity

The links with the prophets and John the Baptist

In ancient times the kings of Israel were called *messiah*. The word means 'anointed one', and from Old Testament times kings and princes were anointed with oil to show that they were 'chosen by God'. The term Messiah, when written with a capital letter, refers specifically to a future leader of the Jewish people whose arrival would bring far-reaching changes to the world. The Jews had long expected a Messiah. The Jewish prophets wrote a great deal about the age of the Messiah, a time when a descendant of King David would usher in a time of peace, a time when God's presence would be felt by all people.

The English word for the Hebrew *Messiah* is 'Christ', in Greek *Christos*.

Matthew's Gospel begins by stating that Jesus, whom Christians call Christ, is indeed this Messiah. He sees the birth of Jesus as a fulfilment of the prophet Isaiah who says in Isaiah 7.13-14:

> Hear then, O house of David ! . . .

> Therefore the Lord himself will give you a sign. Look, the young woman is with child and shall bear a son and shall name him 'Immanuel' [The word 'Immanuel' means 'God with us'].

Matthew uses as his evidence a genealogy linking Jesus, through his family, to the House of David. He begins with Abraham and traces the generations through to Joseph the husband of Mary. Matthew clearly sees the birth of Jesus as a fulfilment of the prophet's words.

Mark, Luke and John concentrate on the story of John the Baptist who heralds the coming of Jesus as the Messiah. According to the Jewish tradition a 'forerunner' would appear to announce the coming of the long-awaited Messiah. This idea, based on the book of Malachi, says that the prophet Elijah will be this 'forerunner'. Instead, the gospel writers all give this title of 'forerunner' to John the Baptist. John, the cousin of Jesus, announces in Matthew 3.11:

> I baptize you with water for repentance but one who is more powerful than I is coming after me; I am not worthy to carry his sandals. He will baptize you with the Holy Spirit and with fire.

In preparation for the arrival of the season of Christmas and a celebration of the birth of Jesus, the Christian Church often uses the liturgical colour of purple for Advent, which is traditionally a penitential colour.

Key ideas . . .
- The beginning of the Christian year.
- Advent is a time of preparation and penitence.
- Christians look forward to the birth of Jesus.

The Bible can help you . . .
- The story of Elijah the forerunner is found in Malachi 4.5-6.
- For Christians the book of Isaiah foretells the birth of Jesus in Isaiah 7.10-16, 9.2-7 and 11.1-10.
- Matthew 1.18-25 tells of Mary fulfilling these prophecies.
- The arrival of John the Baptist is found in Matthew 3, Mark 1, Luke 1 and John 1.

Key words . . .
Venere, forerunner, Messiah.

ACTIVITIES

1 Design an Advent Calendar which focuses on the religious significance of and preparations for Christmas. Explain the reasons for your choice of images.

2 Write a questionnaire about how people prepare for Christmas. Question some friends and family and then examine the religious content of your answers. What conclusions are you able to draw about this important Christian festival?

3 Advent is a good time for Christians to examine their own behaviour, the way they live their lives and the ways of the world. Write a class book of prayers to be used during Advent.

4 Read the prophesy of Isaiah 9.6-7. How do you think Christians might interpret this in the twenty-first century?

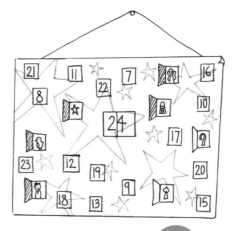

Something to think about . . .

What would be the best piece of good news that you could receive today? Is this something that you just want or is it something that you really need?

Christmas and Epiphany

The major parts of what Christians understand to be the Christmas story are found in two gospels: Matthew and Luke.

Matthew's account

It will help to know . . .

Matthew was a Jew writing for a Jewish audience. The gospel begins with the genealogy of Jesus going back to the time of Abraham and linking Jesus to the house of David through his father Joseph. Matthew is eager to show the birth of Jesus as a fulfilment of the prophets' words.

Joseph's dream

Joseph is central to the opening of Matthew's gospel. Matthew begins his account of the Christmas story with Joseph. Having discovered that Mary, to whom he was betrothed, was with child, Joseph made up his mind to set aside the marriage contract. It was then he was visited by an angel. According to Matthew the angel spoke to Joseph and explained that he should not be afraid to take Mary as his wife and that the child had been conceived by God's 'Holy Spirit'. The story goes on to tell how Joseph did as the angel said and named the child Jesus, meaning 'one who saves'.

It is interesting that Matthew always talks of the angel appearing to Joseph rather than to Mary. Writers of this time were less concerned with women, childhood or adolescence. It was almost as if Mary sat and patiently waited for God to explain things to her betrothed.

Matthew gives no details of the journey to Bethlehem or the birth there; instead he goes straight on in Chapter 2 to the part of the story known as the 'Journey of the Magi', or the Epiphany. The word Epiphany means 'showing forth' and the magi (or astrologers) are the first non-Jews to visit the baby and recognize Jesus' kingship. Matthew includes this visit to show how Jesus had come for all people and not only the Jews. Matthew is the only gospel writer to write about these events and scholars believe that it is Matthew linking the story to the prophecy of Isaiah.

The Christian Church celebrates this festival on 6 January. For the Eastern Orthodox Church it has a special significance, as it is also the day when the birth of Jesus is celebrated.

If you read Matthew's account of this story you will see that he refers to three gifts.

The symbolism of the gifts

Gold: symbolizing kingship. Although a precious and noble metal that does not corrode, at the time of the birth of Jesus gold was less precious than frankincense.

Frankincense: a natural substance gathered from a tree called the Boswellia tree. It was regarded as precious but used to be consumed in great quantities. According to ancient documents the annual consumption of frankincense in the Temple of Baal in Babylon was 2.5 tons.

Frankincense was both functional and philosophical. It was used to embalm corpses but it was also said to have rejuvenating properties with its flesh-preserving qualities (see p. 79).

Myrrh: essence of myrrh also comes from a gum resin which originates in Arabia and Persia and has been used in religious ceremonies since antiquity. The ancient Egyptians called it *phun* and it was used for embalming purposes. Records dating back to BCE 4500 tell of its use. Myrrh has good antiseptic qualities and reduces inflammation. (Today it is often used to treat acne and dermatitis.)

These three gifts are very important as they represent and symbolize the future life and death of this child.

The Escape from Herod

Once the magi had left Joseph, Mary and the baby, Matthew tells how the angel visited Joseph again and told him to take Mary and the baby to safety in Egypt.

Finally after King Herod's death, Matthew tells how the angel appeared to Joseph one last time. In a third dream the angel tells Joseph to return from Egypt with Mary and Jesus. Herod is now dead and the child will be safe.

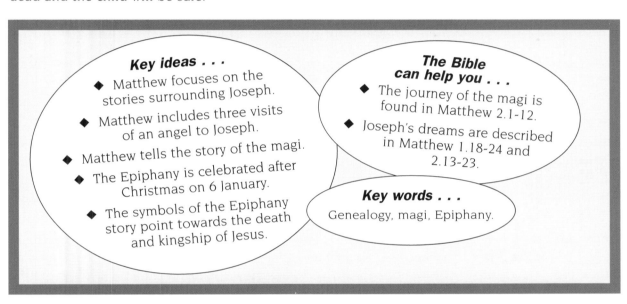

Key ideas . . .
- Matthew focuses on the stories surrounding Joseph.
- Matthew includes three visits of an angel to Joseph.
- Matthew tells the story of the magi.
- The Epiphany is celebrated after Christmas on 6 January.
- The symbols of the Epiphany story point towards the death and kingship of Jesus.

The Bible can help you . . .
- The journey of the magi is found in Matthew 2.1-12.
- Joseph's dreams are described in Matthew 1.18-24 and 2.13-23.

Key words . . .
Genealogy, magi, Epiphany.

ACTIVITIES

1   Find out what you can about Joseph. He only appears once more in Matthew's Gospel account. Can you discover where?

Imagine you are Joseph. Write down a few of your thoughts following your first visit from the angel. What questions might you have asked yourself?

2   Read Matthew 2.1-12. It tells the story of the astrologers' (the magi) visit to the baby Jesus. Find some Christmas cards that depict this journey.

How many astrologers does Matthew say visited the baby?

Do your cards give an accurate picture of the gospel account? If not, why not? Design your own card to give a more accurate account of the story.

3   Explore the Epiphany story in art. Note the relationship that the artist has given to the magi and the baby. You can often find Mary being very protective of her son as the magi kneel presenting the incense and myrrh. Find a famous painting of the Epiphany story and write a poem to express the sentiments revealed in the picture.

Something to think about . . .

If you could have any gift in the world, what would you choose? Would it be a material object or are other things more important?

4   Write a diary account or a newspaper article about this event giving a coherent account of the story.

5   Debate: how would this Jewish family feel receiving a visit and such gifts from these distinguished visitors?

Mark's account

There is nothing of the early life of Jesus in Mark's Gospel. Mark begins his gospel with the baptism of Jesus by John the Baptist and continues with the public ministry of Jesus.

Luke's account

It will help to know . . .

The major part of what Christians understand as the Christmas story of the Nativity is found in Luke.

The Annunciation and Visitation

Luke begins his gospel account with the story of the priest Zechariah and his wife Elizabeth. He tells how Zechariah was visited by the Angel Gabriel who told him that Elizabeth, although barren, would conceive and bear a son. The angel also told Zechariah that they should call the child John.

Luke then goes on to tell how the same Angel Gabriel visited a young woman by the name of Mary. We are not told anything about the background of Mary but we are told that this young woman was 'favoured by God'. The angel tells Mary about her cousin Elizabeth and then said that Mary too would have a child and she must call the child Jesus. This is what Christians refer to as the Annunciation. Luke tells how Mary, having heard the message from the angel, sets off to visit her cousin Elizabeth the wife of Zechariah. It is worth noting that Luke names the angel Gabriel meaning 'God's hero'.

Christians call this meeting between these two cousins the Visitation. Luke's account goes on to describe how the two women, knowing about each other's pregnancy, chant hymns of praise when they meet. The words of Mary found in Luke 1.46-55 are known as the Magnificat. Throughout the centuries, these famous words have been incorporated into Christian worship. They have also been set to music and used as the basis for several hymns. Luke tells how Mary remained with Elizabeth for three months.

The birth of Jesus

The birth narratives of both John the Baptist and Jesus are central to Luke's account.

We find the birth of Jesus, what Christians call the Nativity, in Luke 2.

At the time of Jesus' birth Palestine was ruled over by the Romans. The Jewish people had longed for a strong king like King David. They had hoped that the Messiah would also be a strong and powerful king who could overthrow the Romans and lead them out of Roman occupation.

Luke begins Chapter 2 with the events of the Roman census under the Emperor Augustus. Joseph, being of the House of David, had to return to his family home town of Bethlehem to be registered with Mary. Although like Matthew, Luke is keen to show that Jesus is of the House of David, this gospel talks about Jesus being born in an animal shelter and visited by shepherds, rather than wealthy Jews from important or royal families. Luke is eager to show that the birth of Jesus was for everyone and not just for a privileged few.

The angels in Luke tell the shepherds that they will find the Messiah wrapped in cloth and lying in a manger, a place used for animal food. This was not the traditional Jewish perception of the Messiah. Luke expresses the simplicity of Jesus' birth as opposed to the Jewish expectations of a powerful, kingly Messiah.

Key ideas . . .
- The birth of John the Baptist and Jesus.
- The simplicity of the birth of Jesus.

The Bible can help you . . .
- The story of Zechariah and Elizabeth is found in Luke 1.5-25.
- The visit of the Angel Gabriel to Mary is in Luke 1.26-38.
- Mary's visit to her cousin Elizabeth is found in Luke 1.39-56.
- The traditional nativity story is in Luke 2.1-20.

Key words . . .
Annunciation, Visitation, Messiah.

ACTIVITIES

1   Read Luke 2.1-20. Now compare this story with the traditional nativity scene in the picture below. Try to explain the reasons for the difference.

Something to think about . . .
Why do you think the birth of Jesus is such an important event for Christians?

2   Luke 1.26-28 tells the story of the Annunciation. What do you think the word 'annunciation' means? Do you know any other word that sounds similar? What questions do you think Mary wanted to ask? What do you think Mary thought once the angel had left? Who did Mary tell? Who would you tell if something like this happened to you? Who would believe you? Write Mary's diary account of her experience.

3   Examine a selection of Christmas cards. Find out which gospel/gospels the artists have used for their inspiration. You will note that only Luke includes the visit of the shepherds to the Holy Family.

4   Luke's Gospel tells how Jesus was born in an animal shelter and visited by shepherds, not wealthy Jews from important families. Read Luke 2.15-17. Why do you think Luke included the shepherds when he wrote his story?

5   Find out what celebrations take place in your local church including what liturgical colour is used for the Christmas festival.

John's account

It will help to know . . .

John attempts to show Jesus as someone for all people and for all times. John's Gospel begins with a summary of the Old Testament, from the creation through to the prophets and John the Baptist. He begins 'In the beginning was the Word and the Word was with God and the Word was God'. Jesus' arrival into the world is expressed as 'The Word was made flesh and dwelt among us'.

John describes Jesus as the 'Word of God'. Some prefer to see this idea as God's wisdom – a powerful force which Christians believe called the universe into being and brought order from chaos as well as light from darkness.

Jesus as the light of the world

There is no reference to the traditional nativity story in this gospel. John based his gospel firmly in the theology of the Hebrew Bible (The Old Testament) and devotes the first five verses of his gospel to the coming of Jesus as the Christ, the Messiah. John refers to the birth of Jesus as a light entering the world of darkness.

Key ideas . . .
- John portrays Jesus as the 'Word of God', the *logos* who was there from the beginning of time.
- John the Baptist is shown as the forerunner who prepares the way.
- John refers to Jesus as the light entering a world of darkness.

The Bible can help you . . .
- If you read John 1.1-14 you will see how John has explained the birth of Jesus.

Key words . . .
Light, darkness, Word, *logos*.

Something to think about . . .

Read John 8.12. What do you think this quotation means for Christians today?

ACTIVITIES

1   Read the following verse from the Christmas carol 'O come, all ye faithful':

> Yea, Lord, we greet thee,
> Born this happy morning,
> Jesu, to thee be glory given;
> Word of the Father,
> Now in flesh appearing . . .

You will see that the writer has chosen John's Gospel for his inspiration. Find some other Christmas carols and decide which gospel accounts the writers have used for their inspiration.

2   Read John 1.5-9. Now look at a selection of Christmas cards. Find one that you think reflects these verses in John's Gospel and write a poem to go with it.

3   Begin with a darkened room. Now light a candle. How do you feel now? Discuss. How do you feel in the dark? Discuss your feelings. Close your eyes for a moment and imagine what it would be like to be without sight. What would you miss the most? What would you find difficult to do? Imagine walking around a room or getting dressed in the morning. What problems would you encounter? Are there any other activities that you might find difficult if you could not see? How would you overcome them? Who could you ask to help and why? Discuss the qualities that this person might have and why. Are these qualities important?

Read the words from John's Gospel (1.5-9). What do you think this means? What is John saying about Jesus?

Design a stained-glass window to express John's idea that for Christians Jesus is regarded as the 'light of the world'.

4   Luke 2.25-33 tells the story of the presentation of the child Jesus at the Temple in Jerusalem. Simeon, seeing the baby Jesus, also refers to him as 'a light to lighten the Gentiles'. Gentiles are those who are not Jews. What do you think Luke was trying to say about Jesus?

5   Churches today celebrate Jesus' presentation in the Temple. This event is celebrated on 2 February. One of the names for this day is Candlemas. Can you think why? Find out how this festival is celebrated in a local church.

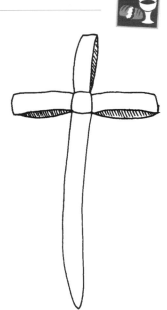

Lent

It will help to know . . .

The purpose of the Lenten season is to prepare Christians for the annual celebration of Easter, a time when they remember the death and Resurrection of Jesus. Although this period of 40 days has become a time for Christians to remember the 40 days and 40 nights that Jesus spent in the wilderness preparing for his ministry, this was not originally the main focus. Christians were initially and still are called to observe Lent as a holy season, a time of self-examination, repentance, prayer, fasting and self-denial.

For Christians today, Lent is a time of new beginnings, a time when they are able to change their ways and make a fresh start. For many

Christians Lent is now regarded as a positive time when they take up new challenges or do something with their lives in order to help others.

Many Christian groups hold regular study groups during this period or use the time to prepare candidates for baptism and confirmation. The liturgical colour is blue, purple or unbleached white.

Ash Wednesday

Ash Wednesday is the first day of Lent and for many Christians it marks the beginning of a time of fasting or self-denial. Many Christians try to 'give up' or fast as a test of their own strength of character. Ash Wednesday marks a stark contrast to the previous day, traditionally known as Shrove Tuesday. In many countries Shrove Tuesday is a day marked by feasting and carnival in preparation for the 40 days which follow. Symbolically, it is a time to use up stored rich food in preparation for the austere time to follow. In Britain we traditionally make pancakes to use up the flour and eggs.

Many churches also 'give up' things, such as flower decorations, in an attempt to change the mood and help members of their congregations enter into the experience of this special time. Parts of the main Eucharist service may also be omitted such as music and singing or saying joyful 'Alleluias'. Vestments and altar frontals are changed to the sombre colour of purple, deep blue or unbleached white. Although it is less common today, some churches still cover statues and crosses as they did when these were often extremely ornate and jewelled.

The imposition of ashes

In many churches another feature of the Ash Wednesday Eucharist is what is called the 'imposition of ashes'. Ashes made by burning the palm crosses and palm branches from the previous year are blessed by the priest and then used to make the sign of the cross on the forehead of each member of the congregation. Special words are said to help the congregation begin their journey through Lent: for example, 'Turn away from sin and be faithful to Christ.'

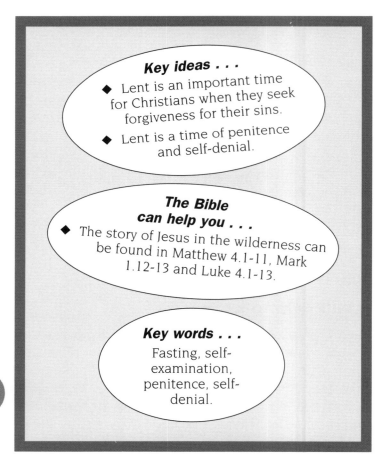

Key ideas . . .
- Lent is an important time for Christians when they seek forgiveness for their sins.
- Lent is a time of penitence and self-denial.

The Bible can help you . . .
- The story of Jesus in the wilderness can be found in Matthew 4.1-11, Mark 1.12-13 and Luke 4.1-13.

Key words . . .
Fasting, self-examination, penitence, self-denial.

Something to think about . . .

Think about times when you have been tempted to do something wrong. Think about some strategies that could help you overcome this temptation.

ACTIVITIES

1 Lent is a time of new beginning. Imagine you are a Christian. Think about the ways in which you might like to change your behaviour during the 40 days of Lent. Write down your thoughts on a piece of paper and seal it in an envelope. After 40 days open it to see if you have had any success.

2 Find out about Shrove Tuesday carnivals that take place in other parts of the world. Sometimes these special days are referred to as Mardi Gras or 'Fat Tuesday'. Produce a class display on these Christian celebrations around the world. You might like to make some of the traditional food and hold a class celebration.

3 Write a class prayer book of 40 prayers, one for each day of Lent.

4 Interview a local priest or members of the Christian community and find out how the different Christian churches in your area keep Ash Wednesday.

Mothering Sunday

It will help to know . . .

Mothering Sunday is celebrated on the fourth Sunday in Lent. It was traditionally a time when the Christian community honoured their mother Church. Christian communities would make the journey from their own parish church to the cathedral, the mother church of the diocese.

During Victorian times when many young girls were working away from home in domestic service it became a special day when they were allowed home to visit their mothers. Today the celebrations have been extended to include three themes: mother Church, Mary the Mother of Jesus and mothers in general. This special day has now become a time when the Christian community considers the role of mothers and offers an opportunity to express both love and thanks for the work that they do.

The services in the church will be as they are for normal Sundays in Lent although the theme of mothers will be dominant. For example, the sermon may be preached on the theme of mothers, and in many parish churches flowers are presented to the children and adults to give to their own mothers.

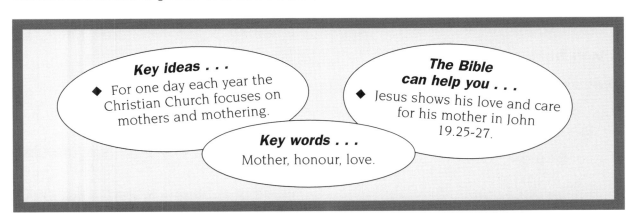

Key ideas . . .
◆ For one day each year the Christian Church focuses on mothers and mothering.

Key words . . .
Mother, honour, love.

The Bible can help you . . .
◆ Jesus shows his love and care for his mother in John 19.25-27.

ACTIVITIES

1   Make a list of five things that you think are important about mothers. Compare your list with a friend's. See if you can agree between you on five key qualities.

2   Devise a Mothers' Day act of worship to hold in your school. Write the prayers, choose the hymns or songs and write an address or short talk about the importance of mothers. You could also include some poems or a dance.

3   Pick out some key events from the life of Mary the mother of Jesus (the Virgin Mary) and design a stained-glass window to depict these. Write the words for a plaque to explain your design.

4   Explore images of the Virgin Mary from religious art across the world. Identify any common features.

5   Imagine you are Mary the mother of Jesus towards the end of her life. Write an autobiography describing some of the most important times in your life and how you felt.

6   The Christian Church has always held the Virgin Mary in great esteem. Interview your local Roman Catholic priest and find out about the particular respect and devotion given to Mary as the mother of Jesus in this Christian tradition.

Something to think about . . .

Think about someone who loves and cares for you. Do you always return this love and care in the same way?

Holy Week and Easter

Introduction

The festival of Easter is the most important of all the festivals for Christians. It celebrates one of the major Christian beliefs: that not only did Jesus die on the cross but he also rose from the dead three days later. This extraordinary story is found in different versions in each gospel. Each account gives details of the last week of Jesus' life, the clashes with the authorities, the arrest, trial, Crucifixion and the Resurrection appearances.

This can be quite an extensive study for pupils so one approach is to focus on the events in one gospel account and then explore the differences in the other gospels. The following section looks at the key events in the story in Mark. The story begins in Mark 11 when Jesus has arrived in Bethany.

It will help to know . . .

The triumphal entry into Jerusalem – what Christians call Palm Sunday

◆   Two of the disciples are sent to find a donkey which Mark describes as a colt.

◆   As Jesus enters Jerusalem crowds spread their cloaks and greenery on the ground.

◆   Some of the crowd wave palm branches and shout 'Hosanna!'

◆   Jesus visits the Temple.

◆   Jesus then returns to Bethany.

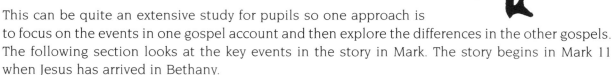

The days before Jesus is arrested

◆ The following day Jesus returns to Jerusalem. On the way, he curses a fig tree.

◆ Jesus drives out of the Temple those changing money and those selling animals for sacrifice.

◆ Jesus challenges the chief priests and the scribes (teachers of the law).

◆ The Jewish authorities begin to seek ways to rid themselves of Jesus.

◆ That evening Jesus returns to Bethany.

◆ The following day Peter notices that the fig tree which Jesus cursed has indeed withered.

◆ Jesus returns to Jerusalem once again and teaches in the Temple.

◆ Once again Jesus' teaching and actions challenge the authorities.

◆ Jesus warns the disciples of his imminent death.

◆ Two days before Passover Jesus is once again in Bethany with his friends.

◆ A woman anoints Jesus' head with perfume.

Passover

◆ Jesus sends two disciples to prepare a room for Passover.

◆ Jesus arrives at the house that evening to join his friends.

◆ Jesus tells of his betrayal to the authorities.

◆ Jesus shares the Passover meal with the disciples during which he blesses and breaks the bread saying 'Take; this is my body' and then takes the cup of wine and says 'This is my blood of the covenant, which is poured out for many'.

◆ Jesus and the disciples go out onto the Mount of Olives.

◆ Peter is told that even he will deny Jesus three times before the end of the evening and before the cock crows twice.

◆ Jesus and the disciples reach the garden of Gethsemane.

◆ Jesus takes Peter, James and John to go and pray.

◆ Jesus asks the three disciples to stay awake and pray while he goes a little further alone.

◆ The disciples are unable to stay awake and fall asleep three times.

The arrest and trial

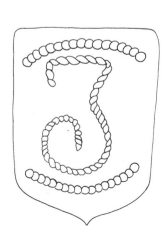

◆ Judas arrives with a crowd armed with swords and cudgels.

◆ Judas betrays Jesus with a kiss.

◆ One of those present cuts off the ear of the High Priest's servant.

◆ A young man tries to run away but his garment is caught and he flees naked (this young man is thought to have been Mark himself).

◆ Jesus is taken to the Jewish authorities.

- Jesus goes on trial.

- Three times Peter denies being a follower of Jesus.

- The following morning Jesus is taken to Pontius Pilate.

- Pilate questions Jesus.

- Pilate offers to release a prisoner for Passover.

- The crowd choose Barabbas.

- Jesus is taken to the Praetorium where he is mocked and beaten.

The Crucifixion

- Jesus is taken to Golgotha to be crucified.

- Simon of Cyrene is given Jesus' cross to carry.

- Jesus is nailed to the cross at 9 o'clock in the morning.

- The Roman guards cast lots for his clothes.

- The inscription above the cross reads 'The King of the Jews'.

- Two robbers are crucified with Jesus.

- Darkness falls at midday and lasts for three hours.

- Jesus utters his last words from the cross 'Eloi, Eloi, lama sabachthani?'

- Jesus is given a sponge of sour wine.

- The centurion watching says 'Truly this man was the son of God.'

- Mark talks of the women being present including Mary Magdalene.

The burial

- Joseph of Arimathaea asks for the body of Jesus.

- Pilate sends for the centurion to confirm the death.

- Pilate agrees that Joseph may have the body.

- Joseph buys a linen sheet and lays the body of Jesus in the tomb.

- The women watch and see where the body is placed.

The Resurrection

- The women return to the tomb (after the Sabbath) to anoint the body with oils and spices.

- The women find the stone rolled away and the body gone.

- A young man dressed in white tells the women not to be afraid and that Jesus has risen from the dead.

- The young man gives the women instructions to go and tell Peter and the disciples.

- The women run away in fear and trembling.

- The women deliver the message to the disciples.

The Resurrection appearances in Mark's account

◆ Jesus appears to Mary Magdalene.

◆ Jesus appears to two disciples who were walking in the country.

◆ Later Jesus appears to the eleven disciples and chides them for their lack of faith

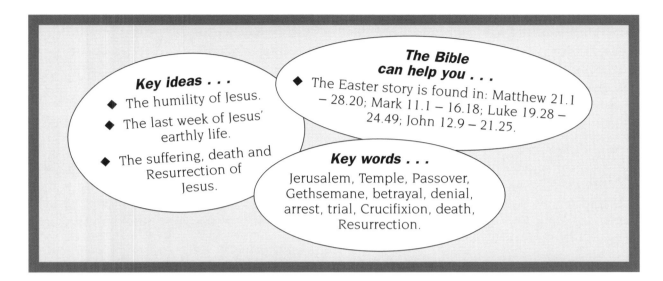

Key ideas . . .
◆ The humility of Jesus.
◆ The last week of Jesus' earthly life.
◆ The suffering, death and Resurrection of Jesus.

The Bible can help you . . .
◆ The Easter story is found in: Matthew 21.1 – 28.20; Mark 11.1 – 16.18; Luke 19.28 – 24.49; John 12.9 – 21.25.

Key words . . .
Jerusalem, Temple, Passover, Gethsemane, betrayal, denial, arrest, trial, Crucifixion, death, Resurrection.

ACTIVITIES

1 Choose one or two sections above from Mark's Gospel and compare his account with that from another gospel: for example, the Last Supper in John 13.4-17 or the visit to Bethany in John 12.1-8.

2 Find a collection of religious paintings with an Easter theme. Try to work out which gospel account the artist has used for his inspiration.

3 Take one section of the Easter story and write an account of the story as if you were there. You may wish to be a reporter and report on the events taking place.

4 Using some of the signs and symbols associated with the Easter story (see pp. 85-8) design an altar frontal or a stained-glass window for Easter.

5 Read the story of the road to Emmaus in Luke 24.13-35. Could this be the journey into the country to which Mark refers (Mark 16.12-13)? Imagine that you are Luke. Write the conversation that you would have with Mark to justify your reason for including this story in your gospel.

6 Find out how a local church celebrates Holy Week and Easter. The following four sections based on the Church of England are designed to help you. You might like to compare these celebrations with a different Christian denomination.

Something to think about . . .

Can you think of a time when you have felt betrayed by your friends? How did you feel? How do you think Jesus felt? Is it hard to forgive?

Palm Sunday

It will help to know . . .

Palm Sunday marks the beginning of Holy Week and the final week of Jesus' life. Christians refer to this as the Passion. It is usually marked by a re-enactment of Jesus' entry into Jerusalem on a donkey when the crowds shouted 'hosanna' and waved palm branches. In many Christian churches the service begins with a procession. The whole congregation gathers at a convenient place and processes towards the church. In most churches palm branches or palm crosses are carried, but Christian churches vary and some simply use the branches from local trees.

In several European countries and towns the Palm Sunday procession becomes an elaborate event with a large procession through the streets. Jesus can be portrayed riding on a donkey and children wave palms and shout 'hosanna'. People gather as the procession moves along and as the tableau moves around the streets, prayers are said, there are readings from the Scriptures and hymns are sung. This marks the start of the Easter story which is about to unfold. Such drama helps to bring this powerful story alive.

For many Christians, Palm Sunday, Maundy Thursday, Good Friday and Easter are like movements in a symphony, if they miss one part they feel unable to gain a full understanding of the whole.

The change of mood

Central to the Palm Sunday celebrations in most Christian churches is the Eucharist or Holy Communion service. During this service the mood changes. The gospel reading of the Passion story is a key part of the Palm Sunday liturgy. It is traditional for different people to read different parts of the story to reflect the nature of the characters. The gospel used is often the Passion story from Matthew, but practice varies. The powerful story of the Crucifixion of Jesus helps to change the mood. The service, having begun with the waving of palms and the joyful shouting of 'hosanna', ends with the cries of 'crucify him'.

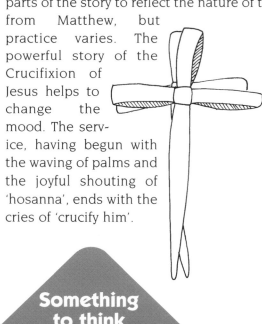

Something to think about . . .

What qualities did Jesus possess that made him so popular with the ordinary people?

Key ideas . . .
- The anticipation of the arrival of the Messiah.
- The excitement of the crowd.
- The humility of Jesus.
- The change of mood.
- How the mood of a crowd can change rapidly.

The Bible can help you . . .
- The Palm Sunday story is found in Matthew 21.1-11, Mark 11.1-10, Luke 19.29-40 and John 12.12-19.
- Matthew's Passion story is in Matthew 26 and 27.

Key words . . .
Hosanna, crucify.

ACTIVITIES

1   Read and compare the events in the four gospels. Make a chart to explore what aspects of the story are found in each gospel.

2   Write a coherent account of Jesus' entry into Jerusalem as if you were there.

3   Write a poem or a hymn for Christians to use in a Palm Sunday service today.

4   Find out what happens in your local Christian community and write a newspaper article either to advertise or to explain these events.

Maundy Thursday

It will help to know . . .

The word 'Maundy' comes from the Latin word for commandment, *mandatum*. This is a special day for Christians. It is the day when they remember the Last Supper, the agony in the garden of Gethsemane and the arrest and trial of Jesus. The Last Supper is a key event for Christians. It was at this Last Supper which Jesus shared with his friends that he changed the words of the traditional Passover meal and commanded his followers to break and eat bread and drink wine in his memory. Christians throughout the world continue to do this. This act of remembrance is known as the Eucharist, Holy Communion, Mass or The Lord's Supper. (see pp. 62–3)

The blessing of oils

As Maundy Thursday commemorates the day when Jesus instituted the Eucharist through the Last Supper, it is also the day on which priests may renew their priestly vows. This service is called the Blessing of Oils and it is one where oil blessed by a bishop is distributed to the priests for them to use in their ministry the following year. Holy oil is used for baptism, confirmation and the anointing of the sick and dying (see pp 59–62, 69–70.)

The distribution of Maundy money

This is an ancient tradition dating from before the Middle Ages. However, when the Church of England broke with the Church in Rome and the English monarch became Supreme Head of the Church in England, the ceremony took on a greater significance.

The reigning monarch, as Head of the Church, gives out special coins, called 'Maundy money', to elderly people at a service on Maundy Thursday. One coin is given for every year of the monarch's age. The coins are silver and are specially minted for the occasion. The service takes place in one of the great English cathedrals and it usually takes 40 years before it is held at the same cathedral again. In the year 2000 the ceremony took place in Lincoln Cathedral and 148 old-age pensioners, 74 men and 74 women, each received the Maundy money. In times past not only were the poor given coins to help provide food but the monarch also washed the recipients' feet.

The Maundy Thursday Eucharist

In some churches this is a very special service. White vestments are worn by the clergy, and members of the congregation are chosen to have their feet washed by the priest. The number chosen is usually twelve to represent the number of disciples. The priest goes to each of the twelve in turn, kneels before them, washing and drying either one or both feet. This is a symbolic gesture to

re-enact Jesus' washing the feet of the disciples at the Last Supper. It is a very powerful symbol, and a deep expression of humility and love.

After the Holy Communion or Eucharist, the remaining consecrated elements may be saved or 'reserved', to be used during a Eucharist on Good Friday. In some churches this bread and wine is transferred to a special altar with a tabernacle. This altar is called an 'altar of repose' and it is usually decorated in a special way with candles and flowers.

When the formal part of the Eucharist service has ended a solemn ceremony begins. As the choir sings or chants a psalm, the candles on the altar are extinguished and the part of the service known as the 'stripping of the altar' begins. Slowly and reverently the vessels, books and artefacts are removed. All altar coverings are taken away and the church lights dimmed. When all is complete and the altar bare, both congregation and priests kneel in silent prayer. Those who wish to leave do so in silence. In many churches this poignant moment is followed by what is known as a 'watch of prayer' perhaps by the altar of repose. Although in most churches today this 'watch' normally ends at midnight some Anglican churches still retain a 'watch' throughout the night to symbolize Jesus' agony in the garden of Gethsemane and his arrest and trial before both the Roman and Jewish authorities.

Key ideas . . .
- Jesus the servant.
- The institution of the Eucharist.
- Betrayal.
- The prayer and agony in the garden of Gethsemane.

The Bible can help you . . .
- You will find the story of the Last Supper in Matthew 26.17-35, Mark 14.12-31, Luke 22.1-38, John 13.1 – 17.26.
- The story of Jesus washing the disciples' feet is found in John 13.1-20.
- The story in the garden of Gethsemane and the arrest and trial is found in Matthew 26.36-75, Mark 14.32-72, Luke 22.39 – 23.12 and John 18.1-40.

Key words . . .
Mandatum, water, oil, humility, love, Eucharist, prayer.

ACTIVITIES

1   Jesus behaved as a servant. Think about some occupations today which could be considered as menial. Explore what might happen if these tasks were not carried out, e.g. cleaning the toilets. Make a list of these important tasks.

2   Find out about the Jewish festival of Passover. What did Jesus say and do that significantly changed this event for Christians?

3   Write a letter to a Jewish child about the significance of the Last Supper for Christians.

Something to think about . . .
Think about ways in which people in power today show examples of humility.

4   Explore the role of Peter in this story. Write a diary account as if you were Peter.

5   Imagine Judas is on trial. Role-play the trial using the courtroom model, e.g. judge, jury, defence, prosecution, witnesses etc.

6   Write the letter that Judas might have left explaining his actions to the other disciples.

7   Write a prayer to be read at a Maundy Thursday service which reflects the feelings of one of the characters involved in events which took place in the garden of Gethsemane.

8   Investigate the role of a priest. Imagine that you are also thinking of becoming a priest. Write a letter to a member of your family explaining the reasons for your decision. Say what aspects of the work you might find difficult and why.

Good Friday

It will help to know . . .

Good Friday is one of the most holy days in the Christian calendar. It is the day that recalls Jesus' journey to the cross and the final hours of his life. Many Christians mark this day by eating hot cross buns and fish. The ingredients in the buns have a special significance. The currants represent the nails, the spices the tears and sadness and the cross the Crucifixion itself. A fish has traditionally been a key Christian symbol which began in the days of the Early Church (see p. 85–6).

Stations of the Cross

Good Friday practice in the Anglican Church is variable. Traditionally many churches hold a simple service of Holy Communion using the bread from the altar of repose, followed by a service of Stations of the Cross. This is followed at 12 noon with a 3-hour service of devotion until three o'clock, the time regarded as the ninth hour when Jesus finally died on the cross. These three hours include prayers, hymns and preaching as well as periods of silence and reflection. The idea of this long service is to symbolize the kneeling at the foot of the cross. For many reasons, often work-related, this length of time has sometimes become impractical and so the services are often rearranged and shortened.

In some churches there is also a procession following a large cross. Once the cross is at the front of the church, the members of the congregation walk to the cross, kneel and kiss the foot of the cross to express their feelings for the sacrifice that Jesus made. This is called 'The Veneration of the Cross' and it is a very moving experience for those involved.

Many Christian communities wish to draw attention to the solemnity of this special day and to witness their faith to all those who regard it as just another Friday. In many countries there is a colourful presentation of this story. Sometimes it is re-enacted in a shopping centre or along a particular route. It is a great moment for street theatre.

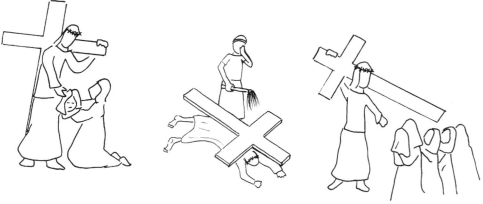

One of the most famous 'Passion plays', as they are called, takes place in Oberammergau in Germany.

As you can see from the pictures there are 14 Stations of the Cross and they represent the final journey of Jesus from being condemned to death to being laid in the tomb. A description of each station is given in Appendix 2 (p. 89), with bible references. In many churches you can see them in art form around the walls of the church. Throughout Lent and on Good Friday these images are used as part of the devotions. Bible readings and prayers are said at each station to help Christians follow the last hours of Jesus' life.

ACTIVITIES

1   Imagine that you are a reporter in the Jerusalem crowd on Good Friday. Write your report about the events that took place and include one or two interviews with some key characters. Try to compare and contrast different viewpoints.

2   Choose one of the Stations of the Cross and write a suitable prayer or poem to be read aloud at this point in a service.

3   Make a class frieze depicting the 14 Stations of the Cross.

4   Using the story from Mark's Gospel, Mark 15.16-47 (see pp. 41–2), write your own version of a Passion play to be acted out in class.

5   Imagine you are the Roman centurion on duty at the Crucifixion of Jesus. Write your report to your commanding officer explaining the events that took place.

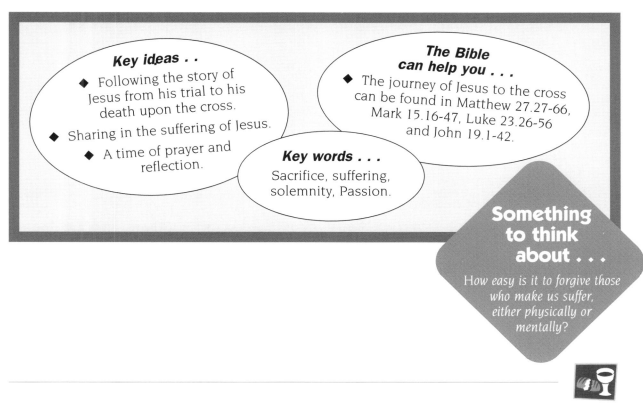

Key ideas . .
- Following the story of Jesus from his trial to his death upon the cross.
- Sharing in the suffering of Jesus.
- A time of prayer and reflection.

Key words . . .
Sacrifice, suffering, solemnity, Passion.

The Bible can help you . . .
- The journey of Jesus to the cross can be found in Matthew 27.27-66, Mark 15.16-47, Luke 23.26-56 and John 19.1-42.

Something to think about . . .
How easy is it to forgive those who make us suffer, either physically or mentally?

Holy Saturday and Easter Day

It will help to know . . .

The use of candles has long been a tradition in both Jewish and Christian worship. The lighting of candles and lamps in church can be traced back to the vigil services held on the eve of the Sabbath. By the fourth century, lamps and candles had become a common feature in Christian worship.

In many churches throughout the world the first Eucharist/Holy Communion of Easter takes place late on Holy Saturday evening or very early on Easter day. This service is called the Easter Liturgy and it consists of four main parts. These parts are intended to form a whole but they can be celebrated separately. The parts are:

A   The Vigil

B   The Service of Light

C   Baptism – The Liturgy of Initiation

D   Holy Communion – The Liturgy of the Eucharist

Customs may vary in local churches but each section is an important component of the Liturgy.

The Vigil

This is the oldest feature of the celebration of Easter and it is a vigil of watching and waiting. In early times the Christian Church would keep a vigil throughout the night, meditating on the acts of God in the Scriptures and praying until dawn when the Resurrection of Jesus was acclaimed. Today the readings will be from the Old and New Testaments and they include the account of Exodus and the Easter story from one of the gospels.

Many churches today continue to hold a short service of readings and prayer before the Service of Light whereas for some the vigil readings from the Old and New Testaments are incorporated into the Service of Light itself. Church of England services usually take one of the following forms:

Form A

    The Vigil

    The Service of Light

    The *Gloria in excelsis*

    The Collect

    A New Testament reading

    A psalm

    The Gospel

    The sermon

    The Liturgy of Initiation

    The baptism and/or confirmations (optional)

    The renewal of baptismal vows

    The intercessions/prayers

    The Liturgy of the Eucharist

Form B

    The Service of Light

    An introduction to the readings

    The Old Testament readings

    The *Gloria in excelsis*

    The Collect

    The New Testament readings

    A psalm

    The Gospel

    The sermon

    The Liturgy of Initiation

    The baptism and/or confirmations (optional)

    The renewal of baptismal vows

    Intercessions/prayers

    The Liturgy of the Eucharist

The Service of Light

In this part of the service the Resurrection of Jesus is proclaimed in the spoken word and drama.

The service usually begins in darkness. The priest then lights and blesses a new fire which is usually lit outside the church for safety reasons. This is known as the paschal fire and from it the priest or deacon lights a special candle the 'paschal candle'. For Christians this candle represents Christ as the light of the world rising from the darkness of the grave.

As you can see from the illustration, this is a large candle which has a deep symbolic significance and is marked in a special way. On it are the Greek letters Alpha and Omega, the first and last letters of the Greek alphabet, which symbolize for Christians that Jesus is 'the first and the last, the beginning and the end'. It also has a cross and five grains of incense pressed into the wax to represent the wounds of Jesus. If you look closely you will see a date. This represents the idea that for Christians Jesus is still present in the world today.

As the candle is lit it is raised up high and the minister sings 'The light of Christ'. Easter has now begun and the candle represents Jesus rising from the dead and overcoming darkness. The candle is carried in procession through the church and from it other candles are lit until the whole church is ablaze with light and each member of the congregation is holding a lighted candle. For Christians this is a very powerful symbol of Christ entering the world as 'A light to lighten the darkness'.

The Liturgy of Initiation

In the early centuries of the Christian Church the sacrament of baptism was linked to the season of Easter. Traditionally this Easter service was the time when people were baptized or confirmed and many churches still use this as the main time for baptism, especially of adults. If a bishop is present then those candidates who have been preparing for confirmation during Lent are also confirmed.

The water for baptism is blessed and baptized members of the congregation also renew their baptismal vows.

The Liturgy of the Eucharist

Following the Liturgy of Initiation there will be the first Eucharist of Easter. The newly confirmed candidates will then receive communion as full members of the Christian Church.

Although this special Easter Vigil takes place in many churches early in the morning, these churches will also hold additional festival services of Holy Communion/Eucharist later during the day. This is to mark what is for Christians the most holy day of the year.

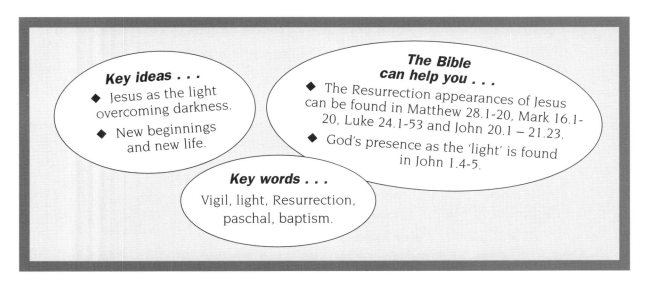

Key ideas . . .
- Jesus as the light overcoming darkness.
- New beginnings and new life.

The Bible can help you . . .
- The Resurrection appearances of Jesus can be found in Matthew 28.1-20, Mark 16.1-20, Luke 24.1-53 and John 20.1 – 21.23.
- God's presence as the 'light' is found in John 1.4-5.

Key words . . .
Vigil, light, Resurrection, paschal, baptism.

ACTIVITIES

1 Compare and contrast the accounts of the resurrection appearances in all four gospels. Consider the particular role of the women in each of the gospel accounts.

2 Write the conversation that might have taken place between the women, following the events in Holy Week.

3 Imagine you are Mary Magdalene. Write your diary account of the first Easter.

4 Design a paschal candle to be used in your local church, using the key events from the Easter story.

5 Interview a local priest or priests about how Easter is celebrated in their church. Using a computer, design a leaflet to inform local people of what happens and the times of the services. You might like to illustrate it with Easter signs and symbols.

Something to think about . . .

How important do you think this story is for Christians? What are your beliefs about life after death?

Ascension

It will help to know . . .

As we grow up we learn to stand on our own two feet. Sometimes we have to leave the people we love. This might be just for a short time, for example starting school, but sometimes it is for much longer periods. Just because people are out of sight it does not mean that we stop loving them or they us.

The gospels tell how after several resurrection appearances Jesus finally left his friends for them to carry on his work alone. No longer was Jesus there in person day-by-day to answer their questions. No longer could they go to him directly and ask for help. From now on they would have to remember all the things that he told them. The disciples were going to have to 'stand on their own two feet'. They were beginning a new adventure alone. Matthew's account tells how Jesus gave the disciples instructions on how to continue without his physical presence.

Christians call this day Ascension Day and it is celebrated 40 days after Easter. The name 'ascension' comes from Mark's and Luke's accounts of this story which tell how Jesus was 'taken up into heaven'; he ascended.

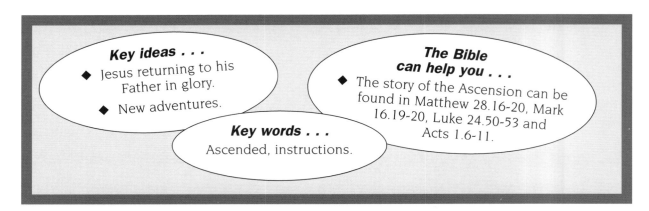

Key ideas . . .
- Jesus returning to his Father in glory.
- New adventures.

Key words . . .
Ascended, instructions.

The Bible can help you . . .
- The story of the Ascension can be found in Matthew 28.16-20, Mark 16.19-20, Luke 24.50-53 and Acts 1.6-11.

ACTIVITIES

1   Look at the words from the bible accounts. What instructions did Jesus give to his disciples? Write the conversation that took place between the disciples as they walked down from the mountain.

2   Compare and contrast the different bible accounts. Imagine that you had been present. Write your own account.

3   There are many things that help Christians remember Jesus. Think what some of these might be. Imagine you were one of Jesus' close friends and write a list of the major events in Jesus' life that will help other Christians remember.

4   Find out how your local church celebrates Ascension Day. Design an order of service to encourage others to attend the service. You might investigate some Ascension Day hymns and write your own prayers.

Something to think about . . .

What would you like people to remember about you?

5   The following words are taken from the second verse of the well-known hymn by W. Chatterton Dix (1837–98), 'Alleluia, sing to Jesus'. Try to explain the meaning and significance for Christians today.

> Alleluia, not as orphans
> Are we left in sorrow now;
> Alleluia, he is near us,
> Faith believes, nor questions how;
> Though the cloud from sight received him
> When the forty days were o'er,
> Shall our hearts forget his promise,
> 'I am with you evermore'?

6   Explore different works of art that depict this event in the gospels. Which one do you think gives the best understanding of the event? Write about your choice.

Pentecost

It will help to know . . .

The Christian Church is born

Pentecost, or Whitsun as it is sometimes known, is the last day of the Easter season. It takes place 50 days after Easter. Pentecost is regarded as the birthday of the Christian Church, the day when the disciples were given the power of the Holy Spirit. We find the story in the Acts of the Apostles Chapter 2. In the Old Testament wind and fire were seen as signs to show that God was present. If you read the story in the book of Acts it talks about the Holy Spirit coming as 'wind' and 'fire'.

The Jewish people had long believed in the power of God at work as being the 'spirit' (see also p. 15). They thought of the spirit of God as 'breath' or 'wind'. The Hebrew word for breath is *ruach* and the Greek word is *pneuma*. Sometimes Christians use the term Holy Ghost instead of Holy Spirit. The Old English word *gast* means the same as 'spirit'. We often say someone has 'given up the ghost' meaning they have died, they 'breathe' no more.

A person filled with the breath of God was said to be filled with life, with 'spirit', a person 'inspired'.

Fire is also an important symbol of power as it can be both a friend and an enemy. It can be a source of heat to keep us warm but it can also be harmful and destructive. The liturgical colour for Pentecost is Red

Something to think about . . .

How do you feel when you are excited or experience something very wonderful?

How would you explain it to someone else?

Key ideas . . .
◆ The power of the Holy Spirit.
◆ The birthday of the Christian Church.
◆ Changed lives.

The Bible can help you . . .
◆ The story of Pentecost can be found in Acts 2.1-13.

Key words . . .
Holy Spirit, power, life, birthday.

ACTIVITIES

1   Explore the symbols used for the Holy Spirit.

Wind, fire and a dove are all examples of symbols used to describe the Holy Spirit. Why do you think these have been chosen as symbols to express the power of God? Write down words to describe the qualities of each.

2   Read the following verse of the hymn 'Come, Holy Ghost, our souls inspire' translated from Latin by John Cosin:

> Come, Holy Ghost, our souls inspire,
>
> And lighten with celestial fire;
>
> Thou the anointing Spirit art,
>
> Who dost thy sevenfold gifts impart.

Find out about the gifts of the Spirit (Romans 12.3-8 and 1 Corinthians 12.4-10). Design a stained-glass window to depict one or more of these gifts.

3   Research the Pentecostal Movement in America and Britain (you could use the Internet). Imagine you are a member of a Pentecostal church. Write a magazine article to explain what happens at one of the services.

4   Look at the picture above. It shows a bishop's mitre. Find out about the role of a bishop, why a mitre is shaped in this way and the times when a bishop wears a mitre.

Ordinary Time (Trinity, The Kingdom Season and Remembrance)

It will help to know . . .

The season of Trinity as written into *The Book of Common Prayer* was the final period of the Church's year from Pentecost through to Advent. Today, in the *Common Worship* calendar, this is called 'Ordinary Time'. The calendar suggests that the Sundays are kept as follows:

Trinity Sunday

The Sundays after Trinity

All Saints' Day – 1 November

The Sundays before Advent ending with The Feast of Christ the King.

There is no seasonal emphasis except that the period between All Saints' Day and the first Sunday in Advent can be observed as a time to celebrate and reflect upon the reign of Christ in earth and heaven. This is sometimes referred to as 'The Kingdom Season' but these four Sundays in November are now actually called Sundays before Advent.

The month of November is also regarded as a special time of remembrance because of the special days that fall within it. They are: All Saints, The Commemoration of the Faithful Departed (All Souls) and Remembrance Sunday.

What is Trinity?

The Trinity helps Christians celebrate one of the key beliefs of Christianity; that God is Father, Son and Holy Spirit.

This doctrine is not found directly in the Bible but is implied throughout the New Testament. The New Testament writers believed that God has a threefold nature. Not only did God reveal himself as Father, Son and Holy Spirit but God is one, Father, Son and Holy Spirit each with an inseparable relationship.

The Christian idea of the Trinity, often referred to as the 'three in one', was written into the creeds of the Early Church (see pp. 4, 21) and is about relationships: the relationship between God, Jesus and the Holy Spirit. The Nicene Creed, which takes its name from the Council of Nicaea in 325, established the teaching that Jesus was fully God just as the Father was fully God. It describes this relationship as follows:

> We believe in the Holy Spirit,
>
> the Lord, the giver of life,
>
> who proceeds from the Father and the Son,
>
> who with the Father and the Son is worshipped and glorified.

John's Gospel refers to Jesus as the 'only begotten Son of the Father', and the other three gospels speak of Jesus as the 'beloved Son'.

For centuries Christians have attempted to explain this very difficult concept. People have said that it is like ice, steam and water, all aspects of the same chemical substance. More than 1,500 years ago, according to legend, St Patrick plucked a shamrock from the ground in an attempt to illustrate it. Many artists have tried to explain this relationship in their paintings. The liturgical colour is green.

Why this special period of the Kingdom?

Although not designated as a specific season, these four Sundays before Advent enable the Christian Church to focus on the Messianic hope of the Old Testament and the coming of the kingdom of Christ as revealed in the New Testament. This period of the year is seen as a way of emphasizing that the weeks leading up to Christmas (including Advent) have a feeling of looking forward with great expectation. It gives the Church more time to watch and wait for the coming of Christ and his kingdom and culminates on the final Sunday before Advent with the Feast of Christ the King. The liturgical colour changes to red.

Why this special period of remembrance?

November was traditionally regarded as the 'month of the dead'. The first day celebrates All Saints. The following day, 2 November, is The Commemoration of the Faithful Departed (All Souls) and Remembrance Day falls on 11 November. The Christian Church first instituted the Feast of All Saints to remember saints and martyrs who went unrecorded and were therefore not honoured by having a special day in the Church's calendar. The liturgical colour is white or gold.

All Souls, on the other hand, was instituted to remember all Christians who have died. Not all were necessarily saints or martyrs, but many tried to lead good Christian lives. The liturgical colour is purple, although red or green may also be used.

Remembrance Sunday was included in the Christian calendar following the atrocities of the First World War to remember all those who gave their lives fighting for the cause of freedom. This day has now been extended to include all British service men and women who have lost their lives in conflicts around the world. Remembrance Day itself is often referred to as 'Poppy Day' because poppies are worn to remember those who died in the First World War (The Flanders fields were said to have been covered in poppies following the carnage). The liturgical colour is red or green.

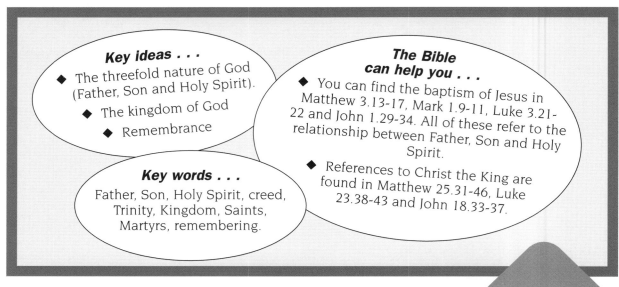

Key ideas . . .
- The threefold nature of God (Father, Son and Holy Spirit).
- The kingdom of God
- Remembrance

Key words . . .
Father, Son, Holy Spirit, creed, Trinity, Kingdom, Saints, Martyrs, remembering.

The Bible can help you . . .
- You can find the baptism of Jesus in Matthew 3.13-17, Mark 1.9-11, Luke 3.21-22 and John 1.29-34. All of these refer to the relationship between Father, Son and Holy Spirit.
- References to Christ the King are found in Matthew 25.31-46, Luke 23.38-43 and John 18.33-37.

Something to think about . . .

What do you think about the Christian idea of the Trinity?

ACTIVITIES

1   Find some photographs of your family. Do you look like any of your family? Sometimes we reflect our family in our behaviour as well as our looks.

   Write down some of the things we know about Jesus. Although Jesus was human, what was it about his personality that made people feel that he was God? Jesus talks about God as Father. Discuss what you understand Jesus meant by saying 'To have seen me is to have seen the Father'?

2   Read Matthew's account of the baptism of Jesus. Design a stained-glass window to depict the concept of the Trinity and explain some of these central beliefs of Christianity.

3   Make a list of words to describe each part of the Trinity. Here are some to help you:

   God – Father, creator, powerful

   Jesus – Son, saviour, teacher

   Holy Spirit – guiding, peace-giving, life-giving.

   Write a poem to express some of these ideas.

4   The following words are taken from a Christian hymn about the Trinity written by Reginald Heber (1783–1826). Write three more verses: one for God, one for Jesus and one for the Holy Spirit. You might use one of the creeds to help you.

> Holy, Holy, Holy! Lord God Almighty!
>
> Early in the morning our song shall rise to thee;
>
> Holy, Holy, Holy! Merciful and mighty!
>
> God in three Persons, blessed Trinity.

5   Read the Lord's Prayer in Matthew 6.9-13. What do you think Christians mean when they say 'your kingdom come, your will be done, on earth as it is in heaven'?

6   Find out which special services take place in your local church during the month of November. Choose either All Saints' Day, All Souls, Remembrance Sunday or the Feast of Christ the King and write an article for a local newspaper explaining why it is important for Christians to remember this day.

The Christian journey through life

Introduction

The sacraments

We all know that electricity exists. We are able to turn on our lights, computers or videos and see electricity at work. However, we are not able to see the electricity, only the effects of its power.

Christians believe that a 'sacrament' is the power of the Holy Spirit at work. It may not be possible to see the power immediately but the results and energy of that power are often clearly visible in people's lives. Just like turning on a light bulb, the power of the Holy Spirit radiates out into the world. Christians reach out to Jesus Christ for power and life to love and live as he did.

All religious traditions have 'rites of passage' which mark important stages on life's journey from birth to death.

For Christians there are seven rites of passage commonly called sacraments. The two major ones are baptism and Holy Communion or Eucharist. These are recognized by all Christians because they were initiated by Jesus himself. The five other rites of passage, Holy Matrimony, confirmation, anointing the sick, ordination and reconciliation, are regarded as sacraments by Christians from the Roman Catholic, Anglican and Orthodox traditions.

A useful definition of a sacrament is an outward and visible sign of something that is inward and spiritual. Each sacrament has its own symbol or sign, something that is outward and visible which helps to provide a simple way of expressing an inner meaning. These are:

◆ water for baptism;

◆ bread and wine for Holy Communion;

◆ rings for Holy Matrimony;

◆ the laying on of hands for confirmation and ordination;

◆ holy oil for anointing the sick and reconciliation.

Although not all Christians will receive all of these sacraments during their lifetime, all will experience the sacrament of baptism.

This chapter explores each of these sacraments and a funeral service based on the practice of the Church of England. A funeral service, which is not in itself a sacrament, marks the final parting from the earthly life as a Christian. Thus a funeral service completes the earthly journey for Christians.

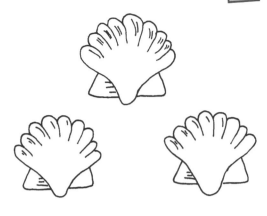

Baptism

It will help to know . . .

The word 'baptism' comes from the Greek word *baptizein*, meaning 'to dip or immerse'. The Jews had baptized people long before Christianity. It had been common practice for Jews to baptize non-Jews (Gentiles) who wished to change direction and become Jews. Jesus' cousin, John the Baptist, had made the Jewish authorities angry because he had called Jews to repent, to give up their sinful ways, and become baptized.

Each gospel tells the story of how Jesus was baptized by John in the river Jordan. Jesus also told the disciples to baptize in the name of God the Father and the Son and the Holy Spirit. Christians have continued to practise baptism as an initiation ceremony into the Church and the Christian family.

From very early times the Church has linked baptism to beginning a new life, starting a new journey, being born again – a fresh start and new journey as a Christian.

The practice of how the baptism takes place will vary greatly among the different Christian traditions, but the common elements will be the use of water as a symbol and the sign of the cross.

The photograph is a picture of the nave roof of Winchester Cathedral. The word 'nave' comes from the Latin word *navis* meaning 'ship'. If you turn the picture upside down you will see that it looks like a ship. When we climb on board a ship we usually begin a journey just as when people become baptized they also begin a journey. This journey however is different from the outward journey that we travel on a ship. This is also an inward, spiritual journey in the Christian faith. Sometimes when we go on a journey on a ship the waters are calm, but sometimes the waters are rough. The spiritual journey is no different, but Christians believe that Jesus will be with them steering the ship so that they need never feel alone.

Church architecture reminds Christians of this journey. As you enter a church you often find a font by the entrance. The font is usually found by the church door to symbolize the fact that at baptism you enter the Christian family. A font is a large bowl that is used for baptism. In some churches these are very large and ornate, whilst in others they are plain and simple. They are all used to hold the water for baptism. The word 'font' comes from the Latin *fons* meaning 'a spring' of water. You can probably see that it is like the word 'fountain'. It is not only babies and young children who begin this journey; adults who wish to join the Christian family are also baptized.

If a baby or young child is baptized it usually has three godparents. These are people who make the baptismal promises on behalf of the child. Their role is to support the parents in bringing up the child in the Christian faith. Once the child is old enough to make these promises for itself then godparents are no longer necessary.

When the promises are made the baptism can take place. In Church of England churches water is poured over the candidate's head three times, in the name of God the Father, Son and Holy Spirit, whereas in other Christian denominations the candidate is totally immersed into the water.

Each tradition would agree that baptism involves four key components:

◆　washing away of sin;

◆　leaving the old way of life;

◆　starting a new life and following Jesus' teachings;

◆　receiving the gift of the Holy Spirit.

Sometimes a scallop shell is used to pour the water over the candidate's head. This is significant because this shell is the symbol of James, the patron saint of pilgrimage or journeys.

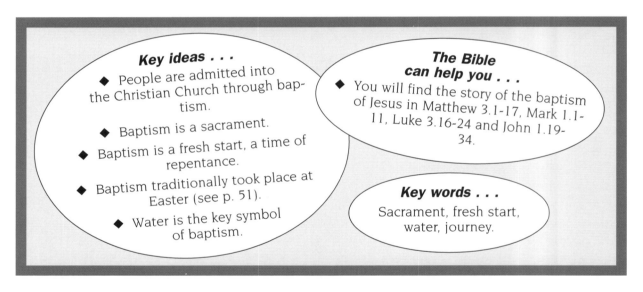

Key ideas . . .
- ◆ People are admitted into the Christian Church through baptism.
- ◆ Baptism is a sacrament.
- ◆ Baptism is a fresh start, a time of repentance.
- ◆ Baptism traditionally took place at Easter (see p. 51).
- ◆ Water is the key symbol of baptism.

The Bible can help you . . .
- ◆ You will find the story of the baptism of Jesus in Matthew 3.1-17, Mark 1.1-11, Luke 3.16-24 and John 1.19-34.

Key words . . .
Sacrament, fresh start, water, journey.

ACTIVITIES

1　Visit your local church and investigate the topic of baptism. You may want to interview the local priest and ask about the order and type of service used.

2　Using an order of service, write a modern baptism service including the key features but adding your own suitable hymns and prayers.

3　Find out about the ways in which different denominations practise baptism. Write a booklet to explain some of these differences to younger children.

4　Imagine that you are a Christian and have recently been baptized. Write a letter to a friend explaining why this was important for you, what happened and how you might have felt.

Something to think about . . .

Can you think of a time in your life when you have felt that the journey was a little rough or perhaps as time when you felt the journey was pleasant and smooth?

Confirmation

It will help to know . . .

For Christians, confirmation is like having their own passport, receiving their own identity as a member of the Christian family. At baptism they are made members of the Christian family but because many people are baptized as children they are unable to make the promises for themselves. Confirmation is an opportunity for the candidate to take on the full responsibility of being a Christian. It is like owning a Christian passport.

If baptism is like birth into the Christian family, then confirmation is like growing up and coming of age. Christians believe that they are given the strength of the Holy Spirit which will enable them to declare publicly their faith as an adult.

Christians who are confirmed are regarded as adults in the Christian Church.

In the Church of England the candidates stand before the bishop who says to the congregation:

> 'Brothers and Sisters I ask you to profess together with these candidates the faith of the Church'
>
> He then says: 'Do you believe and trust in God the Father?'
>
> Candidate: 'I believe and trust in God, the Father Almighty, creator of heaven and earth.'

Once the candidates have been questioned further about their beliefs the bishop confirms them by laying his hands on their heads and saying:

> 'Confirm, O Lord, your servant . . . with your Holy Spirit.'

It is clear that the tradition of 'laying on of hands' in order that someone receive the full strength and power of the Holy Spirit from a bishop dates back to the Early Christian Church.

The word 'confirmation' means 'to strengthen' and during the final prayer the bishop asks the congregation to join with him and say:

> Defend, O Lord, your servants with your heavenly
>
> grace, that they may continue yours for ever
>
> and daily increase in your Holy Spirit
>
> more and more until
>
> they come to your everlasting kingdom. Amen.

Now that the person has been made an adult member of the Christian Church, he or she is able to receive Holy Communion at the Eucharist.

Note:

In recent years there has been much debate about whether children can receive Holy Communion before they are confirmed. In some churches this practice already takes place. It is therefore important that you check the current practice in your local church.

Key ideas . . .
- ◆ Confirmation is a sacrament.
- ◆ This sacrament strengthens and renews the promises made for or by an individual at baptism.
- ◆ Confirmation is about full adult membership of the Christian Church.
- ◆ The power of the Holy Spirit is transmitted through the 'laying on of hands'.

The Bible can help you . . .
- ◆ Acts 8.14-17 tells how Peter and John were sent for in order to lay their hands upon some converts who had been baptized so that they might receive the full power of the Holy Spirit.

Key words . . .
Responsibility, identity, strengthen, 'laying on of hands', Holy Spirit.

ACTIVITIES

1   Imagine that you are a Christian considering the sacrament of confirmation.

   a) Talk to a parish priest about what might be involved.
   b) Write a letter to a friend explaining why you feel confirmation would or would not be a good idea for you.

2   Find out more about the symbols of the Holy Spirit. Design some illustrations for an order of service booklet for a confirmation using one or more of these symbols.

3   Invite someone into your class who has recently been confirmed. Prepare a list of questions that you would like to ask them.

Something to think about . . .

At what age do you think someone is old enough to take on personal responsibility for their own faith?

Eucharist

It will help to know . . .

The night before Jesus died he shared a meal with his friends. Christians call this meal the Last Supper. The gospels tell how during this meal Jesus took the bread, blessed it, broke it into pieces and shared it with his friends saying 'Do this in remembrance of me'. Following this he took wine, blessed it and shared it with his friends saying 'Do this in remembrance of me'. Throughout the centuries Christians from all over the world have followed this command and remembered Jesus with a special meal.

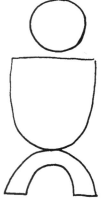

Depending upon the Christian denomination this special meal is called the Eucharist, Holy Communion, Mass or The Lord's Supper.

As Christians share this meal together, they listen to some Bible readings, sing hymns and say prayers. Then just as Jesus did at the Last Supper, the priest takes the bread, blesses it, breaks it and shares it with the congregation. He or she then takes the wine, blesses it and shares that in the same way.

By joining in this meal and sharing the bread and wine in this way the 'family' of the Christian Church not only remembers Jesus but feels able to draw closer to him.

The bread and wine used in the Eucharist help Jesus and his actions come alive for people today. The word 'Eucharist' comes from the Greek word *eucharistia* meaning 'thanksgiving'. Christians say 'thank you' to God for sending Jesus to teach them and show them how to live. They also think about what it means for them to be friends and followers of Jesus.

For many families Sunday lunch is a special time when they all eat together. Others have special meals at Christmas or at other times of celebration when friends or family meet. Christians see themselves as one large family so they too meet together and share this special meal just as Jesus did with his friends. Some Christians call this service 'Holy Communion' because the word 'communion' means 'joining together' and it gives them a sense of unity with one another.

In most Church of England churches the Eucharist or Holy Communion is celebrated at least once a week, but in others this could be every day.

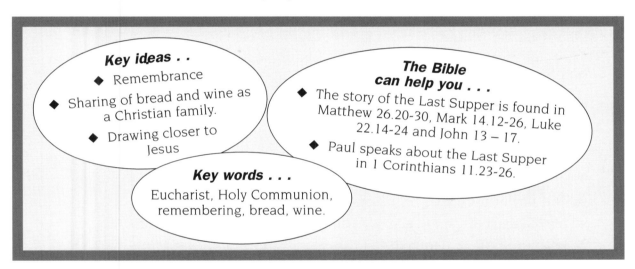

Key ideas . .
◆ Remembrance
◆ Sharing of bread and wine as a Christian family.
◆ Drawing closer to Jesus

Key words . . .
Eucharist, Holy Communion, remembering, bread, wine.

The Bible can help you . . .
◆ The story of the Last Supper is found in Matthew 26.20-30, Mark 14.12-26, Luke 22.14-24 and John 13 – 17.
◆ Paul speaks about the Last Supper in 1 Corinthians 11.23-26.

ACTIVITIES

1   Find out the pattern of services in your local Christian church. Design a leaflet to advertise the services of Eucharist/Holy Communion using suitable Christian symbols.

2   Interview some practising Christians. Find out why they feel the Eucharist is important to them. Using their comments, make a class display entitled 'Christian Eucharist'.

3   Interview a local priest to find out more about the structure of a Eucharist/Holy Communion service. Help write an order of service for a Eucharist to be held in your school or local church for a special celebration of remembering, e.g. leaving your primary school and moving on to a secondary school. Think about some of the things that you would like to say 'thank you' for. You can choose the hymns, write the prayers, choose the Bible readings or design the altar frontal and vestments if they are used.

4   Write a booklet explaining the Eucharist for Key Stage 1 pupils and why it is important for Christians.

Something to think about . . .

Think about someone who is very special to you. How do you/how will you remember them?

Holy Matrimony

It will help to know . . .

Another name for the sacrament of marriage is Holy Matrimony, but we often refer to the ceremony as a wedding.

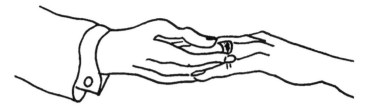

A wedding is a very happy but also a very serious event. When two people love each other they often want to make a lifetime commitment to each other. The most serious part of the ceremony is the making of vows. A vow is an agreement made in the presence of God. It is God that joins the two people together and not the priest. Once the couple have taken their vows they are joined to each other for life. The priest asks the couple:

> The vows you are about to take are to be made in the presence
>> of God,
> who is judge of all and who knows all the secrets of our hearts;
> therefore, if either of you knows a reason why you may not
>> lawfully marry,
> you must declare it now.

During a marriage service the couple also exchange rings. The ring is meant to symbolize unbroken love. In the Church of England the priest says:

> Heavenly Father, by your blessing
> let this ring be to . . . and . . . a symbol of unending love and faithfulness,
> to remind them of the vow and covenant which they have made this day,
> through Jesus Christ Our Lord.
> All **Amen.**

A marriage in church is both a legal and a religious event. The couple sign a document to seal the contract that they have made with each other.

People generally live longer today and a lifetime commitment is for some people very difficult. Some couples grow apart no matter how hard they try. All Christian Churches try to help these couples to be reconciled with each other, but if there is a real problem divorce might be inevitable.

Often these couples then form new relationships and, if they are Christian, they would like to be re-married in a church. Some priests in the Anglican Communion will re-marry divorced couples in church but others feel that having taken vows once, a church blessing is more appropriate.

Although current practice does vary, the Church will try to make this a special time for the couple. Christians today believe that God is understanding and forgiving and would not want people to live in an unhappy relationship.

Key ideas . . .
- Marriage is a sacrament.
- Christian Marriage aims to be a lifetime commitment.

The Bible can help you . . .
- Paul sets out his views on marriage in his Letter to the Ephesians 5.22-33.
- John 2 tells of the first miracle that Jesus performed at the wedding feast at Cana in Galilee.

Key words . . .
Vow, love, commitment.

ACTIVITIES

1 In groups or with a partner, consider the Christian ideal of marriage for life. Write a list of guidelines that you might offer two people considering marriage.

2 Imagine that you are a newspaper reporter. Write about a wedding ceremony that you have seen on a video or attended.

3 Create your own wedding ceremony using your choice of music, prayers and readings.

Something to think about . . .

What sort of person do you think would make an ideal marriage partner and why?

Reconciliation

It will help to know . . .

How many of you have ever broken something made of glass? Glass is fragile, even though today there are techniques to strengthen it and make it safer.

Imagine that you had just broken a very special piece of glass that belonged to a friend or a relative. How would you feel? When we break things that are special it makes us feel very bad about ourselves and we wish that we could 'rewind' the video or put the clock back. Broken glass objects can be put back together but unfortunately they never look as good as they did originally.

Relationships can also be fragile like glass. A hurtful word or gossip can make a special relationship just as difficult to mend. It is not always easy to apologize or admit that we are in the wrong. Christians believe that they have a special relationship with God and throughout their lives they try to do God's will. Sometimes when they make mistakes they feel that it is the same as breaking something very precious and very special and they want to be able to own up and say 'sorry' to God.

When Christians want to say sorry and make amends because they have something on their conscience, they do so in what is called 'confession'. This can take many forms. Sometimes it is part of a service such as the Eucharist but sometimes Christians want to talk about their problems and fears to a priest in a more private way. They want to feel closer to and be 'reconciled' with God.

The sacrament of reconciliation has four main parts:

◆ confession – owning up;

◆ contrition – saying sorry;

◆ absolution – being forgiven;

◆ satisfaction – putting things right.

The conversation is totally confidential, which enables the person to say what is really worrying them or weighing heavily on their conscience. The priest, having listened, then advises and suggests ways of making amends or starting afresh. He or she is then able to give absolution or forgiveness. Words similar to the following might be used:

Almighty God have mercy upon you, forgive you all your sins and bring you to ever-lasting life. Amen.

The final but equally important part of this sacrament is 'satisfaction': being able to put things right.

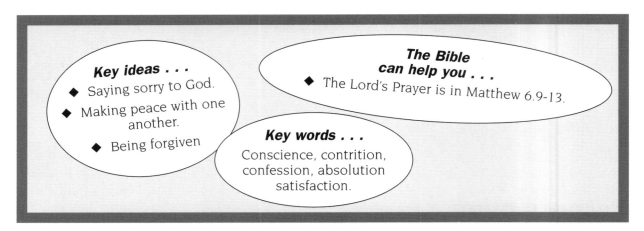

Key ideas . . .
◆ Saying sorry to God.
◆ Making peace with one another.
◆ Being forgiven

The Bible can help you . . .
◆ The Lord's Prayer is in Matthew 6.9-13.

Key words . . .
Conscience, contrition, confession, absolution satisfaction.

ACTIVITIES

1 Can you think of some ways in which you could try to mend a broken relationship?

2 Write a poem about forgiveness and reconciliation.

3 Write a story which is about the four parts of this sacrament.

Something to think about . . .

How do you feel when you do something wrong and then you are forgiven?

Ordination

It will help to know . . .

The word 'church' comes from the Greek word *ecclesia* and it means 'those who have been called'. The word 'ordain' means to appoint 'those who are called' to the Christian ministry. Christians believe that the Holy Spirit is passed on through the laying on of hands at ordination.

The tradition of laying hands on someone's head goes back to the Old Testament when God told Moses to take Joshua and 'lay your hands upon him' to invest him with authority. The Christian Church adopted this tradition as a way of passing on the authority of the Holy Spirit or God's authority. This is sometimes referred to as the Apostolic Succession, the passing on of the Holy Spirit from the time of the apostles.

The word 'apostle' means a messenger, someone who was 'sent out' to tell people the 'Good News' about Jesus. To be classed as an apostle a person had to have seen the risen Jesus.

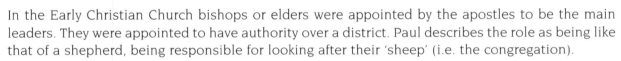

In the Early Christian Church bishops or elders were appointed by the apostles to be the main leaders. They were appointed to have authority over a district. Paul describes the role as being like that of a shepherd, being responsible for looking after their 'sheep' (i.e. the congregation).

The Church of England and the Roman Catholic Church today is made up of bishops, priests, deacons and lay people, but only bishops, priests and deacons are ordained. They are said to be part of an unbroken chain of authority going back to Jesus and the apostles, part of the Apostolic Succession.

Each diocesan bishop is in charge of a 'diocese' (an area based around a cathedral where the bishop has his chair or *cathedra*). Once ordained a bishop has the authority to:

◆ ordain priests and deacons;

◆ administer the Eucharist, Mass, Holy Communion;

◆ pronounce forgiveness of sins;

◆ baptize and confirm new members of the church;

◆ control the finance of the church;

◆ settle matters of dispute.

There are also area and suffragan bishops who are appointed to support and help the diocesan bishop.

Dioceses are also organized into a province which comes under the jurisdiction of an archbishop. The Church of England has the provinces of Canterbury and York. Each diocese is then divided into smaller areas called parishes. The bishop's representative in the parish is called a priest. However, before you can become a priest you have to undergo a period of training as a deacon. This role is one of helper or servant. Deacons assist and support priests today just as the deacons of the Early Church took care of practical matters and supported the apostles, bishops and elders.

The structure of leadership in the free churches is very different because for them all Christians are regarded as having equal status. There are no bishops; instead they have moderators, super-intendents and presidents. These officials have no 'sacramental ministry' and so custom varies as to who can baptize, give Communion and pronounce the forgiveness of sins.

Key ideas . . .

- Bishops, priests and deacons are called by God to do his work.

- The Apostolic Succession is the tradition of passing on the power of the Holy Spirit through the 'laying on of hands'.

- This tradition has been passed down from the apostles and the Early Christian Church.

Key words . . .

Ministry, Apostolic Succession, bishops, priests, deacons.

The Bible can help you . . .

- The story of Moses and Joshua is found in Numbers 27.18.

- Paul talks about his role as an apostle in Romans 1.1-5.

- Paul talks about the role of a shepherd in Acts 20.28.

- The Christian tradition of the 'laying on of hands' is in Acts 13.1-4.

- The appointment by the Church of its first seven deacons is in Acts 6.3-7

- Paul describes the role of a deacon in 1 Timothy 3.8-9.

ACTIVITIES

1 Read the section below. It is taken from the Church of England Service of Ordination to the priesthood:

And now we give you thanks that you have called these your servants, whom we ordain in your name, to share this ministry entrusted to your Church.

Here the bishops and priests lay their hands on the head of each candidate, and the bishop says:

Send down the Holy Spirit upon your servant . . . for the office and work of a priest in your Church.

When the bishop has laid hands on all of them, he continues:

Almighty Father, give to these your servants grace and power to fulfil their ministry among those committed to their charge, to watch over them and care for them; to absolve and bless them in your name, and to proclaim the gospel of your salvation. Set them among your people to offer with them spiritual sacrifices acceptable in your sight and to minister the sacraments of the new covenant. As you have called them to your service, make them worthy of their calling. Give them wisdom and discipline to work faithfully with all their fellow-servants in Christ, that the world may come to know your glory and your love.

Something to think about . . .

Would you like to do the job of a priest? What might you find difficult and what might you enjoy?

The quotation above talks about 'ministry'. Find out about the differences between the role of a bishop, a priest and a deacon. Find out about this word 'ministry' and what it means. You may want to interview a priest and find out what ministry means to them.

2   Find out about the different titles and different roles of the ordained clergy in the Church of England today.

3   Find out about the structure of the Roman Catholic Church. How does it differ from the Church of England?

4   Design and make a stole or some other vestments for an ordination ceremony to reflect the work of a priest.

5   Explore the life of a famous priest, e.g. Thomas Becket, and write a newspaper article about his life.

6   Find out about the leadership of the Free Churches. Write a booklet explaining these roles to someone from another faith.

Anointing the sick

It will help to know . . .

In ancient times the cultivation of olive trees was widespread in the Holy Land. Virtually every village had its own plantation or olive grove.

Olive trees are said to live for many, many years and the oil from the olive tree traditionally has had lots of uses. It was used for the anointing of high priests and other important officials, but its purity and

medicinal qualities meant that it was used to soothe and heal people who were sick. Olive oil was also used to light lamps in people's homes, to cook and to dress salads.

Although olives are very bitter, they can be eaten raw, ripe or unripe. The valuable oil is extracted from the fleshy outer part of the fruit but the seed kernel also contains oil. In Bible times the oil was extracted by pressing the fruit with a vertical round millstone. The crop from a mature tree could produce about 500 kg of oil.

Olive oil is still used for healing by the Christian Church today. This special healing is called 'anointing' or 'holy unction' and people who receive it feel better in mind, body and spirit. Sometimes the soothing effect of the oil eases pain and makes the sick person feel much better.

The oil is taken to people who are sick or very old and the priest anoints them with it. In James chapter 5 we see how he gave instructions about anointing for those people who were sick.

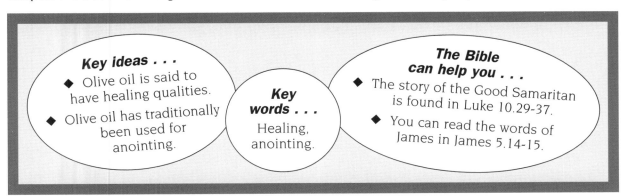

Key ideas . . .
- Olive oil is said to have healing qualities.
- Olive oil has traditionally been used for anointing.

Key words . . .
Healing, anointing.

The Bible can help you . . .
- The story of the Good Samaritan is found in Luke 10.29-37.
- You can read the words of James in James 5.14-15.

ACTIVITIES

1   Write a prayer for a priest to use during the sacrament of anointing.

2   Read the story of the Good Samaritan in Luke then write a modern version of the story.

3   Invite your local priest or deacon in to talk to your class about this sacrament. Prepare some questions in advance.

4   Using the Internet, find out more about the healing properties of olive oil.

5   Read the words of the hymn 'The Lord is my Shepherd'. Using verses 3 and 4 write a poem to convey these sentiments.

6   Explore the ceremonial use of olive oil in the anointing of kings and queens at their coronations, for example, find out about this part of the coronation service for Queen Elizabeth II.

Something to think about . . .

Can you think of some ways in which you might help someone who is sick?

Funeral services

It will help to know . . .

Christians believe that death is the end of our earthly life and the start of a new life where there is the possibility that they will be closer to God in heaven.

The funeral service is a way of saying goodbye and an opportunity to commend their loved ones into God's care for evermore. Although it is naturally a sad time, for Christians it is also a time when the family remembers and celebrates the earthly life of the person. The quotation below is taken from the Christian funeral service.

> 'I am the resurrection, and I am the life,' says the Lord. 'Those who believe in me, even though they die, will live, and everyone who lives and believes in me will never die.'

In the early days of Christianity (see p. 4) people believed certain things about God, and Jesus. By the end of the second century these ideas had been made into a statement of faith or a 'creed' which included reference to Jesus' death and resurrection. For Christians the belief that Jesus overcame death gave them the assurance that they too could experience everlasting life or life after death.

Here is part of the Apostles Creed:

> I believe . . .
>
> The resurrection of the body,
>
> And the life everlasting.

Key ideas . . .
◆ 'Death is the end of earthly life but heralds the possibility of a new life in heaven'.

Key words . . .
Death, resurrection, everlasting life.

The Bible can help you . . .
◆ The funeral service quotation is taken from John 11.25-26.
◆ The resurrection appearances of Jesus can be found in Matthew 28.1-20, Mark 16.1-20, Luke 24.1-53 and John 20.1 – 21.25.

ACTIVITIES

1　Find some photographs of a Victorian funeral like the one below. The photograph was probably taken in the 1890s. What do the photographs tell you about life and religious belief in Victorian times?

2　Look closely at the photograph. You can see that the coffin is covered in flowers. Why do you think people give flowers when someone dies? What qualities do flowers have that make them a suitable gift for such an occasion?

Something to think about . . .
What do you think happens to people when they die?

Where do you think heaven is?

The quotation below comes from a Christian funeral service. Does it give us a clue?

The days of man are but as grass; he flourishes like a flower in a field, when the wind goes over it, it is gone.

3   What do you think the people in the photograph believe happens to a person when they die? If you look closely you will see some flowers in the shape of a cross. Why do you think the cross is such an important symbol for Christians at times of death? Do you think it would be helpful to believe in life after death?

4   Write an order of service for a funeral. Design a cover; consider the music and hymns/songs, prayers, readings and poetry that you would choose to make the service meaningful and a way of expressing the feelings both of thanksgiving for a life shared and of sadness for the separation of death.

A journey to a church

The Church as a living community

It will help to know . . .

When people think of the word 'church' they often think of the building down the road but for Christians the Church is more than that. The word 'church' comes from the Greek word *ecclesia* and it means the whole Christian community. In his letter to the Corinthians, Paul describes the Church as being like a body with different parts making up the whole. This idea of community was very important to the Early Christians and this is still true for Christians today when the community is spread throughout the world. The New Testament not only tells of the birthday of the Church on the day of Pentecost, but also gives information and insight as to how that Church might function. The Church is now and has always been made up of different people, so as time progressed and the Church expanded it became a diverse community. Although the basic truths and principles remained the same, at the level of custom and culture Churches within the Christian community began to reflect differences in practice and organization (see above pp. 21–7).

Today we are left with this legacy. Some denominations have survived while others have lived for a short time and then died. Today the Christian Church is rich in diversity. Practice varies from denomination to denomination and churches are built to accommodate the 'community'; these vary in size and appearance. Some are small and plain while others are huge and richly decorated but each is special for its community and will have something unique to offer.

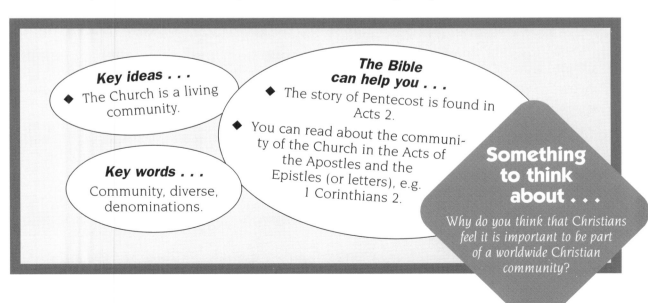

Key ideas . . .
- The Church is a living community.

Key words . . .
Community, diverse, denominations.

The Bible can help you . . .
- The story of Pentecost is found in Acts 2.
- You can read about the community of the Church in the Acts of the Apostles and the Epistles (or letters), e.g. 1 Corinthians 2.

Something to think about . . .
Why do you think that Christians feel it is important to be part of a worldwide Christian community?

ACTIVITIES

1   Interview a member of the clergy or the local Christian community about the importance of the 'Church' today (see also Chapter 2).

2   Find out about the Christian churches in your area. Write a class guidebook for people in another town to explain about your local Christian communities.

3   Choose one Christian denomination and find out about its structure and organization.

A visit to a church

The following section is designed to help teachers plan a visit to the local church. It offers opportunities to explore a church both when it is empty and during worship. The structure is based on the five senses: sight, hearing, smell, touch and taste. It can be used as a way of helping teachers incorporate aspects of spiritual development into their church visit.

Each section offers a selection of ideas but focuses on one area (highlighted in italics). This area has been expanded to show how teachers could develop it in a creative way; other areas are embraced within the activities.

Sight – looking closely

Eyes are very precious; they send pictures to the brain which are stored in our memory. Our eyes are made up of different parts which all work together to help us see. There are also the eyelids and eyelashes which protect the most important parts from dust and too much light. Today we are surrounded by things to see and things to read. Most of the things we learn, we learn through using our eyes. Never before in history have we been open to so many visual stimuli. This can mean that we take our eyesight for granted rather than valuing our sense of sight. For example, before people could read, the Christian Church used stained-glass windows as a means of learning the Scriptures. Some early stained-glass windows are full of detail and symbolism which are often overlooked. When there are many things to see we miss important details unless we look closely.

The empty church
◆   the shape, design and fabric of the building
◆   furniture, e.g. pulpit, lectern
◆   different types of crosses
◆   stained-glass windows
◆   liturgical colours
◆   fabrics, e.g. the altar frontal
◆   vestments
◆   festival decorations, e.g. a crib scene at Christmas or an Easter garden
◆   flowers
◆   candles
◆   carvings and statues
◆   paintings
◆   banners
◆   misericords

During worship

◆ vestments
◆ artefacts
◆ candles
◆ ritual
◆ procession and movement

It will help to know . . .

Misericords

Hidden beneath the tip-up seats in the choir stalls of many English abbeys, priories and cathedrals are some of the most vivid images that have come down to us from the Middle Ages. These are called 'misericords'.

The word 'misericord' comes from the Latin word *misericordia* meaning 'act of mercy'. In the Middle Ages the monks in the monasteries often had to stand to chant or sing for several services a day and sometimes through the night. After a while this became very uncomfortable and so small ledges were placed beneath the tip-up seats to enable the older monks to perch and to take away some of the discomfort as an 'act of mercy'. These were out of sight and the craftsmen felt free to carve all sorts of things on them such as animals, monsters, mermaids and scenes from everyday life.

Sometimes our lives are so busy that we do not stop to look closely and we could easily miss things like these wonderful carvings.

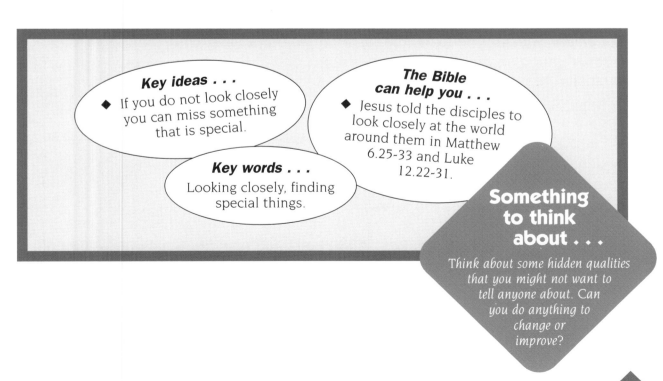

Key ideas . . .
◆ If you do not look closely you can miss something that is special.

Key words . . .
Looking closely, finding special things.

The Bible can help you . . .
◆ Jesus told the disciples to look closely at the world around them in Matthew 6.25-33 and Luke 12.22-31.

Something to think about . . .
Think about some hidden qualities that you might not want to tell anyone about. Can you do anything to change or improve?

ACTIVITIES

1   Find out more about misericords or other special objects that can be overlooked in a church near to you. You might find that the church has a beautifully carved altar, which is hidden from view by the altar cloth, or some interesting stained-glass windows. Write a guidebook about some of these interesting things to see in the church.

2   Our friends may have hidden qualities that we do not see. Just like the misericords these are hidden away but they make people interesting and exciting to know. Ask a friend to tell you two interesting things about himself or herself. Make a class book entitled *Interesting People in our Class.*

3   Throughout history colours have been given special meanings. For example:

◆   intelligence – blue

◆   wisdom – purple

◆   purity – white

Religious traditions have always used colour in this symbolic way. The following list were the colours used in the Church in 1570:

◆   Advent to Christmas Eve   violet/blue/black

◆   Christmas to Epiphany   white/gold

◆   Throughout Lent   veiling of colours

◆   Easter   white/gold

◆   Pentecost   red

◆   apostles, evangelists and martyrs   red

◆   saints other than martyrs   white/gold

◆   baptism/confirmation   white/red

◆   ordination/marriage   white

◆   funerals   violet/blue/black

Explore the use of liturgical colour in your local church today and discover how and where these colours are used.

4   Find out about the life of a famous saint. Using the colours above, design and make an altar frontal and/or a stole to reflect an aspect of the saint's life.

5   Think about your own life. Design a stained-glass window to depict key events from your own life. Think carefully about the colours you choose.

6   Find out more about the different types of crosses used within the Christian tradition.

Visit a local Christian church and see how many different styles of crosses you can find.

Hearing – listening closely

There are three main parts to the ear: the outer ear, the middle ear and the inner ear. The outer and middle ears transmit sounds to the cochlea which is situated in the inner ear. The cochlea is a coiled tube containing millions of sensors which detect sound signals and transmit them to the brain. The sense of hearing is very important. It allows us to communicate with each other and appreciate beautiful sounds, for example music and the sounds of nature. In addition, a sense of hearing can provide warning in times of danger, such as the screech of car tyres.

Throughout the centuries the skill of listening has been an integral part of Christian worship, fellowship and prayer.

The empty church

◆   silence
◆   bells
◆   echoes
◆   the sound of a clock ticking

During worship

◆   liturgy and prayer
◆   chanting
◆   music
◆   responses
◆   readings
◆   hymn singing
◆   silence
◆   bells

It will help to know . . .

Liturgy and prayer

Liturgy and prayer are the foundation of Christian worship. When Christians use the word 'liturgy' they are usually referring to the official prayer that takes place in a church when Christians gather together. Jesus said 'for where two or three are gathered in my name, I am there among them' (Matthew 18.20).

Christian liturgy can include prayer, readings, responses, hymn singing, music and chanting as well as silence and meditation.

Prayer is a special time when Christians feel they come into the presence of and communicate with God.

Some people believe prayer is so important and powerful that they are prepared to dedicate their whole lives to it. These include monks and nuns. Saint Benedict said that the life of a monk was one long prayer and that idleness was the 'enemy of the soul'. Benedict's philosophy was that without study prayer would become repetitive and regimented and without prayer study would lead to pride. By the Middle Ages the monasteries had become great centres for learning and scholarship.

All work throughout the day was to be carried out in the knowledge that God was present. If a monk's life was dedicated to God then he would be punctual, serious and reverent. The *Opus Dei* or 'work of God' was to be the dominating factor and the way of life in the Benedictine monasteries.

Eight times a day the monks were to stop, listen and remember God. In one week the monks would chant the whole book of psalms. This sequence of prayer and worship was called the 'Divine Office' and it still continues in Benedictine monasteries today. It includes the reading of Scripture, the singing of psalms, and the breaking of the bread in the Eucharist. Study is also encouraged in the monastic communities as a means of prayer.

When Cranmer wrote his Prayer Book in 1549–52 for the Church of England, he retained much of Benedict's *Opus Dei*. He ensured that a round of prayer continued day in and day out throughout the year.

Prayer can take many forms. Christians today refer to four main types of prayer:

◆ adoration – praising God for all that is good;

◆ confession – saying sorry to God;

◆ thanksgiving – thanking God;

◆ supplication/intercession – praying for the needs of others.

These prayers can be said or sung out loud, expressed in movement and gestures or silent. Christians believe that prayer is a way of life; it is not always talking to God in a formal setting but being aware that God is always present.

Jesus' own teaching on prayer is found in the gospels of Matthew and Luke. Here we find the most famous prayer for Christians, known as 'The Lord's Prayer'.

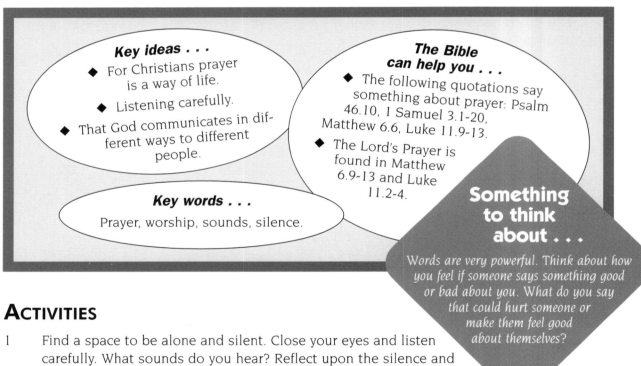

Key ideas . . .
◆ For Christians prayer is a way of life.
◆ Listening carefully.
◆ That God communicates in different ways to different people.

The Bible can help you . . .
◆ The following quotations say something about prayer: Psalm 46.10, 1 Samuel 3.1-20, Matthew 6.6, Luke 11.9-13.
◆ The Lord's Prayer is found in Matthew 6.9-13 and Luke 11.2-4.

Key words . . .
Prayer, worship, sounds, silence.

Something to think about . . .
Words are very powerful. Think about how you feel if someone says something good or bad about you. What do you say that could hurt someone or make them feel good about themselves?

ACTIVITIES

1 Find a space to be alone and silent. Close your eyes and listen carefully. What sounds do you hear? Reflect upon the silence and write down your feelings. Try to write these feelings down as a poem.

2 Read the story of Elijah. It is found in 1 Kings 19.1-18. Part of this story has been put into words in the famous hymn 'Dear Lord and Father of Mankind' by J. G. Whittier (1807–92). The final verse reads:

> Breathe through the heats of our desire
> Thy coolness and thy balm;
> Let sense be dumb, let flesh retire;
> Speak through the earthquake, wind, and fire,
> O still small voice of calm!

What does the story tell about the ways in which God communicates?

3   Listen to a recording of a psalm being chanted. Find a popular psalm, e.g. Psalm 150. Read it quietly to yourself then practise reading it aloud and in time with a partner. Take care to note the punctuation, for example the semi-colons and exclamation marks. Try to pause in the correct places. To help you achieve a good rhythm, pause for one second at the end of each phrase. You must not speak louder than your partner, so you will have to listen very carefully to keep in time.

     If you can manage this task you could try chanting the psalm as a class. Think about how easy or difficult this was. What have you discovered about chanting?

4   Find out more about the life of a religious community of monks or nuns today. Find out about their daily pattern of prayer. Compare this with the custom and practice in a local church. To help you, explore the web site of a monastic community.

5   Make a class prayer tree or book of prayers to use in collective worship.

Smell

The sense of smell is a very powerful sense. The nose contains millions of receptor cells which detect a wide range of smells and then transmit the information to the brain. The receptor cells are so sensitive that in many cases they can detect even a few molecules. For example, some animals detect another animal many miles away. Smells can be evocative, they can alert us to danger, they have the ability to evoke memories and stimulate the appetite. The Christian Church has used always used the sense of smell to enhance worship.

The empty church

- polish and cleaning materials
- old buildings
- old wood
- flowers

During worship

- candles
- incense
- flowers

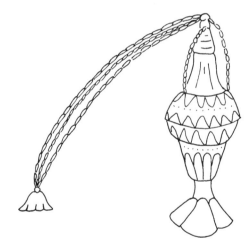

It will help to know . . .

Incense

The ancient world believed that the smoke from incense carried their prayers to heaven and so whatever religious observance was celebrated, incense had to be burned. It was believed to encourage spiritual awareness and expand the consciousness.

Frankincense is a natural substance called 'gum olibanum' which is gathered from the Boswellia tree, a tree found in the hot regions of the world such as North Africa and the Middle East. The best quality frankincense is known as 'Silver Incense' and is produced in Oman. Farm workers place sacking around the base of the trees and cut into the bark to make them 'bleed' for the gum. The gum seeps from the tree and is then left to harden. Once hard, the gum is collected and carried to dealers who grade it according to size. The word 'frank' means 'pure' and this pure frankincense is still used today in aromatherapy, the manufacture of cosmetics and Turkish Delight. Throughout history it has been used for treating respiratory problems, inflammations, wounds and ageing skin. It is known to have flesh-preserving qualities and it was noted that the embalmers of old who used frankincense did not fall prey to the diseases from which their clients had died.

To turn this pure frankincense into incense a number of oils and spices are added to a solution of methylated spirits: 50 millilitres of oil per kilogram of gum.

The recipes for incense have been handed down from generation to generation and costly oils such as jasmine and sandalwood are used. Sometimes up to fourteen ingredients are added and the oil takes between two and fourteen days to dry out.

Incense has always been regarded as something special and holy and it is still used extensively as an aid to prayer and meditation.

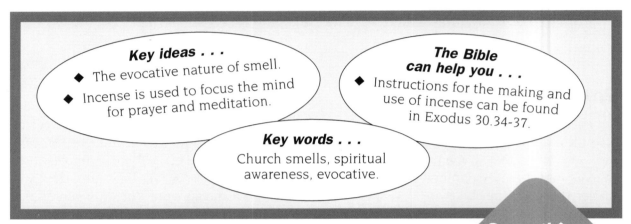

Key ideas . . .
◆ The evocative nature of smell.
◆ Incense is used to focus the mind for prayer and meditation.

Key words . . .
Church smells, spiritual awareness, evocative.

The Bible can help you . . .
◆ Instructions for the making and use of incense can be found in Exodus 30.34-37.

ACTIVITIES

1 Using the Internet, find out how incense is made and used today in Oman (search for Oman).

2 Burn some incense. You will need either some charcoal or an aromatherapy oil burner. Reflect on the smell. Write a poem to express your thoughts and feelings.

3 Find out how incense is used for prayer and meditation in other faiths.

4 Visit your local church. What are its distinctive smells? These may vary depending on whether the building is old or new.

5 Read the following quotation. It comes from a newspaper report on Queen Victoria's funeral in 1901:

> The West door of the chapel was closed, only to be opened for the Heralds preceding the Queen's body and for the Grenadier Guards who were to bear her in, but all up the sides of the steps to that door were walls of wreaths and emblems, pure white for the most part, with many an Irish harp amongst them and here and there deep purple violets. The lower half of the door was screened with huge trophies of flowers, some bearing messages picked out in violets with wreaths of orchids, others of lilies and the chill air was threaded by the scent of flowers. More wreaths were heaped beside the steps and on the grass, with a line of constables guarding the route. It was dark after the daylight, dull though that had been, the colours of the stained glass windows muted by the February gloom, and the scent of flowers was almost overpowering.

Flowers can be a very powerful symbol. The perfume can be very evocative and stimulate the memory. Think about some of the times when we give flowers. If you were to choose a flower to represent your life what would you choose and why? Design a poster to reflect your ideas.

Something to think about . . .

Smells have a powerful way of making you remember special times and places. Think about some smells that evoke a memory for you.

Touch

Inside the skin there are thousands of tiny nerve-endings or receptors. They have special jobs. They detect heat, cold, pain and pressure. These tiny receptors send signals to the brain so that it is possible to know even when a tiny insect is crawling up your arm. Some parts of the body including the hands are particularly sensitive because they have even more receptors.

We use the sense of touch in almost everything we do, often without thinking about it.

Think about some of the things that you touch on a daily basis. You would probably be able to tell the difference between metal or plastic, wood and marble, even with your eyes closed.

The empty church

◆ textures

◆ brass

◆ marble

◆ plastic

◆ metal

◆ wood

During worship

◆ the laying on of hands in confirmation and ordination

◆ anointing

◆ the washing of the feet on Maundy Thursday

◆ the Peace

◆ making the sign of the cross

◆ receiving bread and wine at the Eucharist

It will help to know . . .

The Peace

Besides being very sensitive, hands can also be very expressive. For example, they can radiate strength and weakness.

One important way in which human beings use their hands is when they greet people. Adults generally introduce themselves with a handshake but this is not always easy. It is sometimes difficult to shake hands with someone we do not know or someone we do not like.

Shaking hands can also be a means of reconciliation, a way of saying sorry. The word 'reconcile' means to 'bring back into friendship', to make peace with each other.

Christians believe that it would be wrong to receive Holy Communion as part of the Christian family without being reconciled with each other and feeling at peace with God. During a Eucharist (Holy Communion) the priest invites members of the congregation to share this Peace. This they often do by turning to each other, shaking hands and saying the words 'Peace be with you'. This action is a way of making amends and reconciling themselves with each other. This section of a Holy Communion service Christians call the 'Peace'. The sense of touch is a very powerful symbol.

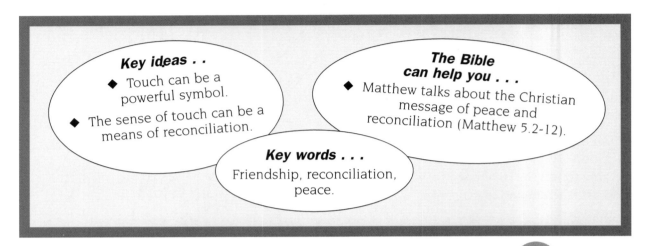

Key ideas . .
- ◆ Touch can be a powerful symbol.
- ◆ The sense of touch can be a means of reconciliation.

Key words . . .
Friendship, reconciliation, peace.

The Bible can help you . . .
- ◆ Matthew talks about the Christian message of peace and reconciliation (Matthew 5.2-12).

ACTIVITIES

1   Go and shake hands with everyone in the class. (Teachers must be sensitive to children from other traditions for whom this might not be appropriate.) Was it easier to shake hands with some people than others? Write down your thoughts having completed the activity.

2   Write a poem or design a poster entitled 'Peace'.

3   Think about a country where there is currently war and strife. Write a letter to a newspaper giving advice on how they could begin to bring about peace with each other.

4   Imagine that you are a member of a local Christian church. Write a letter to a member of another faith community explaining your reasons for including the 'Peace' in your service.

5   Find out about the 'laying on of hands' in confirmation and ordination.

6   Think about the texture of the furniture in your local church. What materials have been used to make the lectern? Are they suitable for the name and style of the building? Could they be more in keeping with the local culture and environment? Thinking about the materials, texture and design, design a lectern to be used in a church near the sea, in the mountains or in an environment of your choice.

Something to think about . . .
Think about your own life. Is there someone with whom you need to make your peace?

Taste

The brain and the tongue work together to help you taste. The tongue is covered with thousands of taste buds which can detect four different tastes: sweet, salty, sour and bitter. This important sense enables us to appreciate a wide variety of foods and to distinguish between good and bad substances. Some insects such as bees and butterflies are sensitive to even minute amounts of sugar. This helps them to find food.

The empty church

Although there are no obvious links to taste in an empty church, representations of food have been important Christian symbols throughout the centuries. These can stimulate discussions on taste:

◆ symbols of bread and wine

◆ food depicted in stained-glass windows

◆ food depicted in carvings

◆ harvest festival displays

During worship

◆ bread

◆ wine

◆ water

It will help to know . . .

Bread

For ordinary people food, warmth and clothing have always been their major concerns. In the days of the Bible the main sources of food were cereal crops, fruit and vegetables. For this reason enemies attacked during the crop-growing season because they knew if the crops were destroyed the people could not survive. Unreliable rainfall, drought and pests all made crops and harvests uncertain.

Wheat and barley for bread-making were grown in the fertile lands around Nazareth, indeed bread was the basic item in every diet. The word 'diet' comes from the Greek word *diaita* meaning 'way of life'. Barley bread was the most common but wheat gave the best flour. Matthew's gospel explains how 40 litres of flour were mixed with water or olive oil to form a dough. As fresh yeast was not always readily available, a piece of fermented dough was usually saved. This was called the 'leaven' and it was kneaded into the new dough to help it rise. Before this was baked, another piece of dough was put aside for the following day. This bread would then be baked as flat bread.

Growing up in Galilee, Jesus knew how important bread was to the community. Matthew and Luke show how Jesus uses bread in the Lord's Prayer to mean 'that food which helps people survive'.

The gospels tell how Jesus referred to himself as the 'living bread'. John tells how Jesus spoke of himself as the 'bread of life' and all the gospels tell how Jesus used the symbol of bread to describe his own body at the Last Supper.

Key ideas . . .
- The importance of bread in sustaining life.
- Jesus uses the symbol of bread to refer to himself.

Key words . . .
Friendship, reconciliation, peace.

The Bible can help you . . .
- Jesus describes himself as the 'bread of life' in John 6.32-36.
- You can find the Lord's Prayer in Matthew 6.9-13 and Luke 11.2-4.
- Matthew describes the kingdom of heaven as yeast in Matthew 13.33.
- The Last Supper is found in Matthew 26.26-30, Mark 14.22-26, Luke 22.14-20 and 1 Corinthians 11.23-35.

Something to think about . . .
Imagine life without being able to taste. What would be some of the special tastes that you would miss?

ACTIVITIES

1   Find a recipe and bake some bread. What happens when the yeast is added?

    Now read John 6.48. Why do you think John refers to Jesus as 'the bread of life'?

2   Find the words of one or more of the following hymns or songs. What do they say about Jesus being the bread of life? How do you think these words help Christians understand more about Jesus?

    'Bread of Heaven, on thee we feed' by J. Conder;
    'Broken for me, Broken for you' by J. Lunt;
    'I am the bread of life' by S. Toolan;
    'Take, eat, this is my body' by P. Simmons;
    'With this Bread' by G. Baker.

3   Compare Matthew's and Luke's versions of the Lord's Prayer. Design a booklet to help explain this prayer to younger children.

4   There are seven sacred species of tree mentioned in the Bible.

    Five of them are fruit trees: the vine, the pomegranate, the palm, the fig and the olive. Find out what the others are and why they are so important in Jewish and Christian belief. You might like to taste the fruits and write a poem about those tastes or design a stained-glass window to represent them.

Appendix 1

Christian signs and symbols

Advent

The scroll depicts the announcement of the birth of Jesus. The Latin words *Ecce Virgo concipiet et pariet Filium* mean 'Lo, a Virgin shall conceive and bring forth a son'.

Ascension

This symbol is used for the Ascension and depicts a flaming chariot or more simply a flaming wheel. This is also used as the symbol for the prophet Elijah (2 Kings 2.1-12). The symbol is a link between the Old Testament and the New Testament and reflects the fact that Elijah also ascended into heaven.

Candles

When lit, a candle reminds Christians of Jesus' words 'I am the light of the world'. Throughout history candles have been used to reflect God's presence in a world of darkness.

Chalice and paten

These are the two key symbols in a eucharistic service. They are simply the cup and the plate for holding the bread and wine during a service.

Chi-rho

This stands for the first and second letters of the word 'Christ' (*Christos* in Greek).

Christmas star

The star symbolizes the journey taken by the magi in Matthew's account of the Christmas story.

The crib

The custom of making a Christmas crib is widespread. In many churches and elsewhere a model is made of the Christ Child in the manger, together with figures representing Mary, Joseph, the shepherds and the magi. The crib is known as the *praesepe* or manger, a place for animal foods. Was this perhaps for Christians a foretaste of what was to come? One day the child would give his body and blood to be eaten in Holy Communion. Often the Christmas cribs in churches create a tableau of the Christmas story as described by Matthew and Luke. One of the most famous is that of the Church of St Maria Maggiore in Rome.

The empty tomb

This has always been a symbol of the Resurrection. It reminds Christians of Jesus overcoming death and rising from the tomb on Easter Day.

Fish

The Greek word for 'fish' was ΙΧΘΥΣ, pronounced ichthus. The letters became a code for the early Christians:

I	Iesous	Jesus
X	Christos	Christ
Θ	Theou	God's
Y	Yios	Son
Σ	Soter	Saviour

During the persecution of the Early Christian Church the fish was chosen as a secret sign. One person would draw the outline of a fish on the ground in the dust or the sand and if the other person was also a Christian they would add the eye.

Gethsemane

This image is called the 'Symbol of Gethsemane'. It shows a chalice, which is usually in gold, and a silver cross on a violet background.

Hot cross buns

Hot cross buns have a special symbolic meaning for Christians. They help to tell the story of the Crucifixion. The currants represent the nails, the cross the Crucifixion and the spices reflect not only the smells of the time but also the tears and sadness of the event.

Icons

An icon is a sacred work of art. It is painted as a form of prayer and meditation. The icon is perceived as a window. The perspective is back to front so that the observer looks through the icon as if to heaven.

INRI

These are the initial Latin letters for **I**ESUS **N**AZARENUS **R**EX **I**UDAEORUM 'Jesus of Nazareth King of the Jews' as recorded in John 19.19.

John

This ancient symbol of a rising eagle reflects the fact that John's Gospel gazed deeper and further into the mysteries of heaven. The symbol is portrayed as a gold eagle on a blue background.

Judas

This emblem shows the 30 pieces of silver for which Judas betrayed Jesus and the rope with which he hanged himself. It is usually shown with a straw-coloured rope on a black background.

Luke

Luke's Gospel deals with the sacrificial aspects of Jesus' life. His emblem is the winged ox, often shown as gold on a red background.

Madonna and child

The Christian Church sees the role of Mary as unique. Mary has always been held as an example to the faithful for the way in which she fully and responsibly accepted the will of God even though at times this would have been very difficult for her. Although Mary's influence and importance varies greatly among the various Christian denominations, for all Christians she portrays that deep love a mother has for her child.

Mark

Mark's Gospel concentrates on the royal dignity of Jesus. Mark's symbol is the winged lion. This is again portrayed as gold on a red background. Some of the most famous images of this are to be found in St Mark's Square in Venice.

Matthew

Matthew's Gospel teaches about the human nature of Jesus. For this reason his emblem is that of the 'divine man'. This image is often portrayed as gold on a red background.

Maundy Thursday

The bowl and the water reflect the washing of the disciples' feet recorded in John's account of the Last Supper.

The *menorah*

Light is an ancient symbol of God's presence. The Temple in Jerusalem had a seven-branched candlestick. This was called a *menorah* and was always kept burning as a symbol of God's continuing presence. It has continued to be an important symbol of the Jewish people.

The mitre

A mitre is the hat worn by a bishop and its shape is meant to represent the tongues of fire referred to in Acts 2.3.

The olive branch

The olive branch has traditionally been the sign of peace and reconciliation. The oldest biblical reference to the olive tree is in the story of Noah when the dove returned with an olive branch as a final proof that the waters had subsided.

The fruits of the tree are fairly large, oval in shape and when ripe are black or dark blue in colour. The valuable oil is extracted from the fleshy outer part of the fruit but the seed kernel also contains oil.

Palm cross

Branches from palm trees are used as symbols of the triumphal entry of Jesus into Jerusalem on Palm Sunday. Each year in many Christian churches crosses made from palm leaves are distributed. They represent the fate that was to befall Jesus. In some Christian churches these palm crosses are then returned the following year and burnt to provide the ashes for the Ash Wednesday services.

Palm Sunday

The palm stands for spiritual victory and the martyr's triumph over death. On Palm Sunday palms reflect Jesus' triumphal entry into Jerusalem and his triumph over death upon the cross.

The paschal candle

For Christians this candle symbolizes the resurrected Christ who has overcome the darkness of the world.

Paul

Paul's symbol is often shown as two crossed swords, however this is also a famous emblem and depicts the 'Sword of the Spirit' as a white book open, with black and red letters. The sword is silver with a gold hilt and on a red background. Tradition tells us that Paul being a Roman citizen was beheaded rather than crucified. The sword also reflects this form of punishment.

Pentecost

There are many symbols that represent Pentecost. One reflects the tongues of flame referred to in Acts 2. Another is the dove which has always been a key symbol to represent the Holy Spirit. It represents the power of God at work in the world and is generally thought to be taken from the gospel accounts of the baptism of Jesus. The dove is usually depicted descending.

Peter

Peter's symbol shows an upside-down cross and crossed keys. Peter was not a Roman citizen and therefore his punishment could be crucifixion. Tradition, however, says that Peter felt unworthy to be crucified in the same way as Jesus and so asked to be crucified upside down. The keys refer to the passage in Matthew 16.19 where Jesus is said to give Peter the keys to the kingdom of heaven.

Pomegranate

This fruit is native to the Mediterranean and the lands of the Bible and it is mentioned many times in the Old Testament. The fruit was used as a sacred symbol in ancient times and because of its many seeds it has become an emblem of fertility and life. When it is used as a symbol of immortality and resurrection it is shown bursting open to expose the seeds. For Christians it has consequently become a symbol of Christ bursting open the tomb and overcoming death.

The scallop shell

Scallop shells have often been used to pour the water over the candidate's head in a baptism service. This type of shell is also the symbol of James the patron saint of Spain and of pilgrims. James is mentioned as the first of the disciples to go on a missionary journey. For Christians baptism is the start of their Christian journey.

Stole

This is worn around the shoulders like a scarf as the name suggests. Traditionally it represented the towel of a servant. A deacon wears a stole across the chest but once he or she is made a priest the stole hangs around the neck in parallel lines.

Thurible

The thurible or censer is used in many Christian churches as a means of burning incense. Charcoal is lit and placed in the bowl of the thurible; then the grains of incense are added. As the thurible is swung it keeps the charcoal burning and enables the smoke and perfume from the incense to pervade the atmosphere.

Trinity

A common symbol for the Trinity is the equilateral triangle. The image depicts the Christian belief in the threefold nature of God. Threefold figures such as the three fishes and the three interwoven circles are also key symbols of the Trinity.

Wedding ring

The symbol of unbroken and unending love given during a marriage service.

Appendix 2

Stations of the Cross (see p. 48)

(see p. 48)

N.B. Those without Bible references are traditional – there is no evidence for them in the Bible.

1. Jesus is condemned to death.

   Matthew 27.15-26

   Mark 15.6-15

   Luke 23.15-19

2. Jesus receives his cross

   John 19.17

3. Jesus falls for the first time.

4. Jesus meets his mother

   John 19.25-7

5. Simon of Cyrene helps Jesus carry his cross

   Matthew 27.32

   Mark 15.21

   Luke 23.26

6. Veronica wipes the face of Jesus

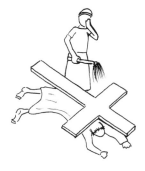

7. Jesus falls a second time

8. Jesus comforts the women who cry.

   Luke 23.27-31

9. Jesus falls a third
time.

10. Jesus is stripped.
    Matthew 27.28-31
    Mark 15.16-20

11. Jesus is nailed to the
    cross
    Matthew 27.33-5
    Mark 15.24
    Luke 23.33
    John 19.23

12. Jesus dies on the cross
    Matthew 27.45-46
    Mark 15.33-41
    Luke 23.44-49
    John 19.28-30

13. Jesus' body is taken
    down and laid in his
    mother's arms.

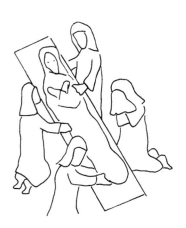

14. Jesus is laid in the tomb
    Matthew 27.57-61
    Mark 15.42-47
    Luke 23.50-56
    John 19.31-42

Appendix 3

Resources

A journey through the gospels

Margaret Cooling, *Using the Bible in Literacy Teaching*, The Stapleford Centre, 1999.

M. Doney, *How the Bible Came to Us*, Lion, 1997.

John Drane, The Bible World Series, Lion, 1996.

J. Priestley, *Bible Stories for Classroom and Assembly*, *New Testament*, RMEP, 1992.

Collections of re-told Bible stories

The Lion Children's Bible, Lion, 1991.

The Graphic Bible, Lion, 1998.

The Children's Illustrated Bible, Dorling Kindersley, 1994.

The Tabloid Bible, Westminster John Knox Press, 1999.

A journey through the Church past and present

B. Brown and A. Melrose, Story Keepers Series, Cassell, 1996 (also available on video).

Margaret Cooling, Faith in History Series, Eagle, 1995.

C. Gibb, *Church and People*, Wayland, 1996.

T. Triggs, *Religion: Tudors and Stuarts*, Wayland, 1993.

A journey through the Church year

Teaching RE Series, CEM, explores major events in the Christian year, e.g. Easter, Christmas, Pentecost, Harvest.

A World of Festivals Series, Evans, 1997.

Nicola Currie and Jean Thomson, *Seasons Saints and Sticky Tape*, National Society/Church House Publishing, 1992.

A. Hunt, *The Tale of Three Trees*, Lion, 1994.

D. Self, *High Days and Holidays*, Lion, 1993.

L. Broadbent and J. Thompson, *Festivals*, Folens, 1994.

The Christian journey through life

Judith Etherington, *Bridges to Religions: The Warwick RE Project*, *Meeting Christians Books 1 & 2*, Heinemann, 1996.

R. Holmwood, *Living Religions: Christianity Part 2*, Nelson, 1996.

D. Rose, Christianity Photopack, Folens, 1995.

A journey to a church

Alan Brown and Alison Seaman, *Christian Church*, A&C Black, 1997.

Lois Rock, *Discovering Churches*, Lion, 1995.

L. Broadbent, Places of Worship Resource Pack, BBC Education, 1997.

L. Broadbent and J. Thompson, *Places of Worship*, Folens, 1995.

General resources

Sister Wendy Beckett, *Sister Wendy's Nativity and Life of Christ*, Rose Publishing, 1998.

Clare Donovan, *The Winchester Bible*, The British Library/Winchester Cathedral, 1993.

David Farmer, *The Oxford Dictionary of Saints*, Oxford University Press, 1987.

Mike Harding, A *Little Book of Misericords*, Autumn Press, 1998.

Michael Perham, *Liturgy Pastoral and Parochial*, SPCK, 1984.

Daan Smit, *Plants of the Bible*, Lion, 1992.

Audio-visual/posters

Testament: the Bible in Animation, BBC.

Story Keepers, Paternoster.

D. Lazenby (ed.), *Eggshells and Thunderbolts*, BBC/Culham.

Images of Jesus Poster Packs, Modern and Traditional, The National Society.

Christians' Poster Pack, Birmingham Regional RE Centre, Westhill, Birmingham.

Easter, Christmas and Christianity Worldwide, Poster Packs, CEM.

Living Religious Poster Pack 1 & 2, Nelson.

Easter, Christmas and Christianity Worldwide, Poster Packs, CEM.

Living Religions Poster Pack 1 & 2, Nelson.

'Inspire' Poster Pack, Winchester/Salisbury Diocese.

Christianity Today, The Story of the Bible, Birth Rites, Festivals, all available from Pictorial Charts Educational Trust.

For further information about resources for teaching Christianity, or for details of publishers and suppliers of RE resources, contact The National Society's RE Centre, 36 Causton Street, London SW1P 4AU, Tel: 020 7932 1190/1, Fax: 020 7932 1199, or email: nsrec@dial.pipex.com.

Information is also available on the National Society's web site at: www.natsoc.org.uk.